Karl Keating

Jeremiah's Lament

RASSELAS
HOUSE

Published by Rasselas House
El Cajon, California

RasselasHouse.com

Cover Design by Damonza.com

ISBN 978-1-942596-07-3 Paperback
ISBN 978-1-942596-08-0 Digital

Contents

Preface

For many, the best way to reach an understanding of the Catholic Church is to see how other people misunderstand it. This book is full of misunderstandings. The people quoted in these pages came to their confusions in various ways. Sometimes it was by reading the wrong books or by failing to read the right books. Sometimes it was a matter of heredity, with prejudices passed down from father to son and from mother to daughter. At other times errors were imbibed at the foot of the pulpit, in the university lecture hall, or from door-to-door missionaries.

Whatever their origin, misunderstandings are misunderstandings. They should be recognized for what they are and set aside, even if that means a break from personal habit or family tradition. More than a century ago, Pope Leo XIII noted that there is nothing so salutary as to understand the world as it really is. That is true particularly of the Church that Christ established because to misunderstand her is to misunderstand him.

The Roman System Way

A subscriber to the magazine I once edited wrote to tell us she didn't need answers from Catholics any longer:

> God's Word, the Bible, has become exactly that to me! I've found without a doubt his Word is all I need! He causes me to grow as I study it and sit under good Bible preaching where everyone brings a Bible to follow along as he compares Scripture to Scripture! When I accepted the Lord Jesus as my personal Lord and Savior, I had no intention leaving "Holy Mother the Church"—in fact, I thought now I'll be like the others and know the what, where, and why of it all. …
>
> And then I started listening to the priest at Mass, and I could see I would have to choose one or the other: the Bible way or the Roman system's way. The answer is obvious. Then, when I got together with the parish priest, he told me I was too fanatic about the Bible! I replied, "Thank you for the compliment." What more did I need? ... No more literature, please.

Reading between the lines, you can imagine what happened. The story is a common one. This woman found no intellectual fulfillment at her parish. Probably, like many parishes, it was just coasting, and she was a once-a-week Catholic. Then a Protestant friend invited her to a service at the neighborhood born-again church. At first our correspondent put her off. Going seemed a bit disloyal, and what did Bible thumpers have to offer anyway? (All she knew about born-agains she had gathered from reruns of *Elmer Gantry*.)

But her friend kept pestering her, in a gentle way, and finally she consented. I'll sit through it once, she thought, and that will be it. Well, it certainly was it—it was just what she was looking for. She discovered "good Bible preaching." Here was a minister who spoke her language, convicted her of sin, and seemed to have the Bible memorized. He was at once blunt in condemnation of the easy, quasi-Christian life she had been living and had been satisfied with (more or less) and encouraging in his eagerness that Christianity be extended to all.

What's more, he didn't look or sound like Elmer Gantry. He didn't wear polyester or a leisure suit, and he didn't wear expensive suits either. He didn't look like a huckster, a nerd, or a con artist. He had a soothing voice and could speak (how to describe it?) not professionally (he wasn't polished or slick), but honestly, from the heart. He wouldn't be mistaken for a scholar, but he clearly was a believer. And he was friendly. After the service her friend introduced her to the minister, and he introduced her to others at the small church. At her home parish there was a rigorous anonymity. You could attend for years and be recognized as a regular, but no one would know your name. Here, at this small church, everyone seemed to know everyone.

That's how it all started. She was invited to join a Bible study class. Why not? she thought. She dusted off the family Bible and went, but soon put it aside and purchased a King James Version so she could read along with the others. She was surprised to find she enjoyed reading the Bible, and she read it often. At the Bible study she at first bristled when people said the Bible supported this or that doctrine—doctrines opposed to what the Catholic Church taught. It wasn't that they bad-mouthed Catholicism as such. Actually, Catholicism hardly ever came up. Instead, it was pointed out to her that peculiarly Protestant doctrines were true, and by implication peculiarly Catholic ones weren't.

She read, for instance, about the "brethren of the Lord." She always had thought these were Jesus' cousins, but everyone at the Bible study insisted they were his brothers-german. What they said seemed to make sense. At least she didn't have anything to say on behalf of the Catholic position. (Of course, she didn't really know what the Catholic position was based on, so she should have expected it to seem inadequate.)

So it went. Week after week she attended both Mass and the Protestant service, and she joined in the Bible study. She became convinced that everything to be believed must be found plainly on the face of the Bible. The Bible was written for simple people, she was told, so there couldn't be a need to draw out tendentious inferences. She realized, after a while, that she was happier attending the Bible study or the Protestant service than attending Mass. The priest didn't have much to say anyhow, just a lot of banal comments about political issues in which she took no interest (never—to her, a telling point—any comments about sin).

Then came the hard sell, though she didn't see it as such. Her new friends explained that Catholicism isn't really Christianity as Christ intended it. Instead, it's a religious *system.* That means it's a scheme through which you effect your own salvation by doing things: going to Mass, taking Communion, going to confession, getting indulgences, praying to statues, and so on. You either choose the Bible way or the Roman system way, she was told.

By this time she knew where her affections lay—she simply liked the Protestants more than the Catholics, the minister more than the priest—and it seemed her beliefs were moving in the same direction as her feelings. She thought she'd give the Catholic Church one last chance. She made an appointment to see her pastor and wasn't surprised that he didn't even know her name, though she had been in the parish for years. She explained to him her devotion to the Bible and how, so far as she could see, all Christian truths are to be found in the Bible and anything not obviously in the Bible is to be rejected. It's the Bible or nothing, she said. If the Bible is true, it couldn't be incomplete. There couldn't be a need for anything else. Now, what do you have to say to *that,* Father?

He said something about her putting a wrong emphasis on the Bible, about not having a right appreciation of Christianity and its history. What he meant, she thought, was that she was a fanatic. It had to seem so to him—after all, *he* never preached from the Bible. Maybe he never even read it, except for those readings at Mass.

Their meeting was short. He was in a hurry, and she was uncomfortable. When she got home she knew what she had to do. It was like when her husband died. After a while, she gathered up things that reminded her of him and threw them away. She did the same with things that reminded her of Catholicism. Gone from the wall was the crucifix, to the trash went the pamphlets and books she had accumulated (not many, and mostly unread), and the rosary she hid in the attic, along with the Catholic Bible. She wrote a few letters, telling people, "no more literature, please." And that was that.

Such is my reconstruction of what is behind the letter. Decide for yourself whether it's a likely scenario. What is sure is that it's a common one. Not that I get many letters like this woman's—in fact, hers was the first ever from a subscriber who was bidding a fond farewell to Rome—but what she went through many people go through. Notice the progression. It begins with dissatisfaction at the parish. The practice of one's faith is nothing more than a once-a-week thing: leave home for

5

Mass, back within an hour. Then comes an invitation to visit an Evangelical or Fundamentalist church. At first the invitation is declined; eventually it's accepted: "just this one time." The friendliness of the congregation and the speaking skills of the preacher seem impressive compared to what is found at Mass, where few parishioners know one another, where the priest does his best (and too often succeeds) in trivializing the liturgy.

So the first impression of Evangelicalism or Fundamentalism is of Evangelicals or Fundamentalists, and the impression is positive. There is a certain attraction, and it's all at the emotional level. The Catholic is willing to let himself be indoctrinated (in the good sense of having doctrine poured into him, not in the bad sense of being brainwashed), and he is a little surprised to discover the new doctrines taking hold. He shouldn't be. They're being poured into a largely empty vessel. They do not have to displace by force of logic any pre-existing doctrines, because what Catholic doctrines already are there are held only at a juvenile level. The Catholic never was catechized as an adult, and his sixth-grade understandings are pushed aside easily by the new doctrines he is meeting now.

That is the positive side of indoctrination. The negative consists of arguments against Catholicism. The Catholic—now half Catholic, half Protestant—has no intellectual defenses. He has nothing to say. He isn't browbeaten into accepting conclusions that are unflattering to Catholicism—what can he do *but* accept them, given that he's never heard any explanation or defense of the Catholic side? Yes, along the way he swallows a lot of unclear thinking and even some outright nonsense, but not consciously. It all seems to fit together.

So he finds himself making that one last trip to the rectory. For many people who leave the Church, it's both the first and last time they speak with a priest. The priest, as often as not, doesn't appreciate the stakes. He doesn't know it's make or break. This isn't always the case, of course. There are many priests who are on their toes, see what's coming, and say all the right things, bringing their inquirers back into the faith. There are others who don't, usually because they don't see the warning signs, sometimes because they do but just don't care.

When the waverer leaves the rectory, he may be a waverer no longer. His worst suspicions may be confirmed ("Good Lord! That priest doesn't know anything about the Bible!"), and he quietly slips away. He makes no fuss, carries no picket signs. He just stops going to Mass and turns all his attention to his new faith.

The Only Game in Town

As recently as the early 1980s, anti-Catholicism was thought to be dead in the United States. Most pundits attributed its demise to John F. Kennedy's campaign pledge, made before Protestant ministers in Texas, that he would not let his Catholicism influence his decisions as President. But anti-Catholicism had already been on the wane for a generation. Its gradual disappearance coincided with the lessening influence of Fundamentalism and Evangelicalism, which met the social gospel in battle during the first decades of the century, and lost. When the social gospel later dissolved into secularism with a religious face, people again turned to Fundamentalist and Evangelical churches because they seemed to be the only ones willing to proclaim that doctrinal truth matters.

Except in the South, where there have never been many Catholics, it is common to find that as many as half the congregants of these churches got where they are by "un-poping." This perhaps explains why many professional anti-Catholics—those who actually make a living at it—had once been loyal to Rome. But not all. For every Bartholomew Brewer—the former Carmelite priest and later Baptist minister who founded Mission to Catholics International—there is a Bob Jones, latest in a line of Catholic baiters and chancellor of a private university in South Carolina that bears his and his forebears' name.

The techniques vary widely. Jack Chick, one of those curiosities for which Southern California is famous, distributes in large quantities comic books depicting Romish intrigues as revealed by a man who claims to have been a Jesuit assigned to subvert Protestantism. These comics have received a lot of play in the Catholic press, but they are far less influential than other anti-Catholic material. They are so grotesque in their charges that even other opponents of the Church have written against their use.

The most effective propaganda confronts Catholics, and those who anyway would be suspicious of Catholicism, with questions that seem to be damning. They seem so because American Catholics are remarkably ignorant of their faith and are baffled by even the simplest questions. This should not surprise anyone who has taught a class of teen-aged confirmands and found that not one knew the Lord's Prayer, even though it is prayed each Sunday at Mass. When Catholics go to their priests for answers to these questions, as often as not they come away disillusioned. Instead of frank and reasonable replies they are given lame excuses such as "because that's what we believe" or, worse, are told that the Church no longer believes that anyway. One hardly can blame people for leaving a Church whose pastors are unable to resolve problems that in fact have straightforward and satisfying solutions.

It is these questions that are swelling Fundamentalist and Evangelical ranks across America. The people in the pews are hungry for doctrinal truth. They have been brought up on scientific dogmas and expect yes-or-no answers in religion also. The answers they seek are more satisfying than the attitude that insists that it isn't polite to talk about religion at cocktail parties or in church.

How many Catholics have left St. Miscellanius's for Good Book Baptist? It's hard to say. Some televangelists claim that more than a third of their viewers (and therefore contributors) are Catholics, and many of those Catholics are gradually disengaging themselves from Rome. Newsletters from anti-Catholic organizations are full of testimonials from people who have seen the light and who have been successful in coaxing their friends to join the exodus.

9

A rough figure? Certainly several hundreds of thousands over the last three decades and perhaps over a million. Although there are said to be more than seventy million Catholics in the United States, many do not practice the faith and are Catholics only in the cultural sense. True, most of the dropouts in recent years have dropped into indifference, not Bible-thumpery, but there is a growing disenchantment even among them with the lack of moorings, and the tract pushers are making considerable headway.

No annual reports are issued by the anti-Catholic groups, so it is hard to say just how much their presses turn out, but the number is surely in the multiple millions. In anti-Catholic talks given in Fundamentalist churches, congregants first are tantalized by ogling a table loaded with Catholic artifacts—prayer books, scapulars, rosaries, holy cards, statues, vestments, even a chalice filled with what one hopes are unconsecrated hosts. The talks are on the need to evangelize Catholics and make real Christians out of them. The outcome is often the founding of a committee to distribute tracts outside Catholic churches and to confront Catholics with the plain truth of the Bible.

So far there seems to be little appreciation at the higher levels of the Church in America that something is going on that should serve as a lesson. There is a real need being met by the Fundamentalists and Evangelicals, and it is not just that they are better at glad-handing than are Catholics. The key is that they are talking about doctrines. That they are confused on doctrinal matters is not the point. The point is that, given the lethargy of the Church here, to many Americans they are looking like the only game in town.

Argument by Sneer

The most unbalanced—at least the most sneering—contribution to the book *Fundamentalism Today* is by Robert W. Shinn, professor of religion and philosophy at Eastern College in Pennsylvania. His essay is titled "Fundamentalism as a Case of Arrested Development." His thesis is that Fundamentalism (and, by implication, orthodox Christianity of any persuasion, including the Catholic) is low on the scale of religious maturity. Shinn recounts and gladly accepts the ideas of James Fowler, who wrote *Stages of Faith: The Psychology of Human Development and the Quest for Meaning.* Fowler, a Methodist minister, relied heavily on the ideas of Lawrence Kohlberg, famous for his thesis that there are stages of moral maturity, with liberals like Kohlberg being near the top, believers in the Ten Commandments toward the bottom. What Kohlberg did for morality, Fowler did for religion, and Shinn proposes to tell us about it.

He begins by noting that, "according to Fowler, faith is an innate primal response and trust in ultimate reality." This definition of faith has nothing to do with the Christian notion, of course, whether Protestant or Catholic. The Protestant's fiduciary faith and the Catholic's confessional faith are quite distinct. Shinn, with Fowler, notes that "all of us grow morally, socially, and educationally in different ways and at different rates. Can it be that the religious dimension is exempt from this growth process?" Of course not. Six stages can be identified, it is said, and here they are:

Stage 1. Intuitive-projective (ages 4 to 8): Here we see the "rise of imagination" and the "formation of images of the numinous and an ultimate environment."

Stage 2. Mythical-literal (ages 8 to 12): This is character-ized by "the rise of narrative and the forming of stories of faith."

Stage 3. Synthetic-conventional (from puberty onward, "sometimes for a lifetime"): The key here is "the forming of identity and the shaping of personal faith." This is the level most Fundamentalists find themselves; by implication, the av-erage Catholic is here too. Note the disparaging "conventional." What Joe Average believes is conventional; what university professors believe, even if they march in lockstep, is not.

Stage 4. Individual-reflective (late teens to middle age): This level features the "reflective construction of an ideology" and the "formation of a vocational dream." You can sense by the phrasing that this level, like the previous one, is for hoi polloi.

Stage 5. Paradoxical-consolidative (midlife and beyond): Here we get to "paradox, depth, recognition of mystery, and responsibility for the world." The religious liberal, whose faith may be reduced to social action, feels at home here.

Stage 6. Universalist ("occasionally with maturity"): "A state reached by rare individuals who identify with humanity with exceptional sensitivity." Shinn and Fowler, with due modesty, do not seem to put themselves in stage 6, being con-tent, apparently, with the previous level.

What of Fundamentalists? "Fundamentalism manifests characteristics of stage 3. In a more enlightened form or phase, commonly called Evangelicalism, it manifests a few of the characteristics of stage 4." (Thomas Howard, a serious scholar and writer, a convert to Catholicism, a one-time Evangelical and professor at an Evangelical college, and the author of *Evangelical is Not Enough*—a plea for a more liturgical Evan-gelicalism, written before his conversion—might be amused to find that he spent most of his adult life mainly in stage 3, but partly in stage 4.)

It should be said in his defense that Shinn notes that these stages are not clear divisions. "Characteristics from different stages can co-exist in any stage. Sometimes people are caught in a very prolonged transition between stages, thereby defying classification." Not to worry. For the most part, we can pigeonhole people easily, particularly folks whose beliefs we don't like.

In stage 3 "adolescents reach out to 'find themselves' and interpret their lives through others in the community, such as those in their peer group, school, or vocation." (Adolescents have vocations?) "Childhood images of God may deepen through some experience or a distinct conversion. Children may find the God who knows and accepts them. As the adolescent participates in society, his fervent religiosity finds expression in a system of beliefs and values from a church, synagogue, youth organization, or Bible club. This is the stage at which foundations can be laid for continued growth. The traditions of believing groups can become real, and individuals can think for themselves." But many never do think for themselves, says Shinn. "There are both youths and adults who are satisfied with a system that answers most or all of their questions and [that] provides the satisfaction of an 'in-group' that screens all 'reality' for them. Association with a group can be a good experience. The strength orthodoxy provides is a cohesive force in any group."

We can agree with this to a certain extent, but Christianity is reduced to psychology. You're a Christian because you can't stand on your own. You can't face "real" reality, so you need a group to manufacture a different reality for you. "With stage 4 people shift from relying on conventional authorities to taking personal responsibility for their commitments, lifestyle, beliefs, and attitudes." It's hard to escape the sense that this implies our religious maturity can be measured by the extent to which we form our faith in our own likeness.

What about religious authority? Shinn explains that "in stage 2 the Holy Bible is a very special book, God's Book, Mother's Book." (Mother's Book?) "Children can be in awe of it as a household fetish. In stage 3 the Bible is an authority that provides God's truth. At a naïve level the Bible and all its contents are sacred." (Take that, St. Jerome!) "Therefore, you honor the Bible and God. At a more sophisticated level the Bible is the authority for conduct and belief. It is infallible or inerrant." Catholics disagree with Fundamentalists about the status of the Bible—we don't believe in *sola scriptura*—but we can sympathize with Fundamentalists whose religion is being travestied here. We're only halfway up the ladder, and already we're on the verge of dropping the Bible as an authority.

A story Shinn relates is revealing. He tells of a professor who, "in a public lecture at Eastern College, reminisced somewhat bitterly about a very early period in her life when she had been indoctrinated by an ultra-conservative Protestant sect, a wing of the Plymouth Brethren. Her perception of reality was to words and expressions taken directly from the King James Bible and enforced as God's very words. Everything was screened through this verbiage, she said, and it took her years to get free of it. Stage 2 was preventing the growth of even a systematic theology characteristic of stage 3." But was liberation to be found? Yes, thank God. "Having wrestled with feminist theology and the study of the nature of God's attributes"—that is, having discovered he is a she—the professor "testifies to her recognition and appreciation of divine mystery in relation to the finitude of all human systems and language patterns." That means she now believes we can't know anything definite about God, so creeds are a waste of time. This is how Shinn characterizes this version of the Pilgrim's Progress: "What a testimony to the sobering influence of a stage 5 transcendence of any and all neatly packaged systems that limit openness to all aspects of a given subject." There seems to be, for Shinn and for his mentor, Fowler, a definite correlation between disbelief and religious maturity. Traditional Christians can be such only because they haven't advanced very far; people who have left Christianity behind are on the road to nirvana.

Shinn feels a bit sorry for people stuck in stage 4. Such "interpreters of the Bible may have to give lip service to creedal, institutional statements about infallibility or inerrancy that are officially binding upon them. Such statements of faith are often linked to seminaries, colleges, or denominations, but scholars in these institutions engage in historical-critical studies that if consistently pursued could cause them to march off the map of rigid, orthodox formulations of the nature and authority of the Bible. ... For stage 3 conservatives such freedom of inquiry is dangerous indeed." The reader is being told, and none too subtly, that truth is to be found among college instructors of a properly liberated bent. And the Catholic reader is told, if he reads between the lines, that it is a good thing not to give anything more than "lip service to creedal" statements.

There is another problem here, says Shinn. Stage 3 thinking, even stage 4 thinking, is intellectually dishonest. If you're a thinker at all, and if you stay at these levels, you're just faking it. "A stage 5 friend of mine who has been through the mill of persecution blames his experiences on blind obedience to the dogma of a Perfect Book. He looks back ruefully to a time when he himself taught Scripture and 'defended the Word of God' with elaborate chicanery, artful dodges, and legerdemain. He gradually grew through stages in which inner freedom, peace, and joy were his, totally harmonious with a serious appropriation of critical biblical scholarship. He longs to join hands and heart with Evangelicals of pre-critical understandings, but their fear of such new learning makes that impossible."

What a sustained sneer! Catholics can criticize Evangelicalism's approach to the Bible—we can, and we do—but what Catholic would suggest that Evangelicals' arguments defending their interpretations of the Bible are little more than "elaborate chicanery, artful dodges, and legerdemain"? Notice how Shinn's friend matured through acceptance of "critical biblical scholarship." Now true scholarship with respect to the Bible has always been fostered by the Catholic Church. So often "critical biblical scholarship" is nothing but a phrase meaning rejection of the Bible as inspired and in any way authoritative. When it means that, it usually also signals a palpable failing of the intellect, a kind of despair that reason can attain truth.

Did Shinn's friend enjoy an "inner freedom"? Quite possibly. There is the freedom that comes with an acknowledgement of and obedience to truth, and there is the freedom (or, we should say, the simulacrum or ghost of freedom) that seems to come with abandoning truth and the search for it. When we free ourselves that way, we take comfort in looking down on people of "pre-critical understandings."

Shinn doesn't seem as sure of the uniqueness of Christianity as he once may have been. He says, "The simplistic devices used in stage 3 and too often in stage 4 cause the 'true believer' to respond to world religions as if they were toys or idols. The range and vitality of Asiatic religions, for example, may be misrepresented, underestimated, and maligned." True, as far as it goes. But then he goes too far. "The world religions compete with Christians at whatever stage they are. Unfortunately, in even the most broadminded writings of stage 4 scholars, non-Christian religions are described abstractly. There is no effort to cultivate an in-depth sensitivity to the riches and depths of understanding and devotion the sophisticated author-teachers of those religions represent. The in-group aggressive resistance to building bridges of understanding and tolerance has been called 'tribalism,' a term probably most popularized by that stage 5 Baptist theologian, Harvey Cox." Cox, of course, was for years the epitome of the liberal Protestant.

It's correct that many believing Christians don't appreciate the elements of truth to be found in non-Christian religions. This occurs because no investigation has been made, either from lack of time or lack of interest. After all, it's sensible for a convinced Christian—someone convinced Christianity is true and that no important religious truth can be found *only* outside Christianity—to put the study of Eastern religions on the back burner. The busy astronomer will study the Copernican system and its modern offshoots because he is convinced they describe accurately the movements of the planets and stars. Only if he has free time or a particular curiosity will he learn the inner workings of the Ptolemaic system. Granted, there are "riches and depths of understanding" in that geocentric theory, but also error and confusion. Is an astronomer to be called enlightened because he declines to prefer Copernicus to Ptolemy? Call such an astronomer what you will—but don't call him in to do the calculations for the next satellite launch.

"If levels suggest a ladder of ascent, Fowler has said he would object to the picture." Yes, but that may be what needs to be said for public consumption. The fact is that Fowler's six stages, as discussed by Shinn, are supposed to be stages of improvement. Higher is better. After all, notes Shinn, Fowler "clearly favors the sophistication and scope of outlook found at stages 5 and 6. These last two stages can be linked to the highest understandings of the theme of the kingdom of God." Of course, that's the view of people who are in stage 5 and 6. Folks stuck at stages 3 and 4 might think Fowler's ladder doesn't go straight up, but, like a two-sided step ladder, up and down: up to stages 3 and 4, then, on the other side, down to stages 5 and 6. After all, a good argument can be made that the chucking of Christianity is a sign of diminishing faculties, not maturing ones.

Shinn says those "who have grown into later, more advanced ... stages must not become condescending toward those in earlier stages"—but he says this after writing the most condescending essay in *Fundamentalism Today.* But that is to be expected from a man whose final paragraph reads this way: "Fundamentalism is a pejorative term—in it is no health or healing. If more churches were centers of therapeutic growth, some traits of reactionary conservatism could be overcome and growth could be encouraged without painful or traumatic transitions."

The truth is that Fundamentalism is not—or should not be—a pejorative term. It can be used legitimately to describe conservative Protestants who share many doctrines with orthodox Catholics. Although we differ with Fundamentalists on many points, there is a (partial) community of belief. Let's pray we can better understand them as we try to make them understand us, and let's all pray, Catholics and Fundamentalists, that people such as Robert W. Shinn learn that discussion by sneer is not the way to go.

Two Notions of Worship

Here's a pop quiz my I have given in parish seminars: "You recall that the Israelites melted down their jewelry and made a golden calf. What was wrong with making a golden calf?" Before anyone has a chance to embarrass himself publicly, I give the answer: "Absolutely nothing."

When I ask that question and give that answer, most people are stunned. "But we know making the golden calf was a sin," they say. "The Israelites were condemned for it." Actually, my listeners know no such thing. There wasn't anything at all wrong with fashioning a statue from jewelry. What was wrong was that the Israelites then worshiped the non-existent god the calf represented. They committed the sin of idolatry. There never has been a sin of statue-making.

"But God expressly forbids making statues," say many Fundamentalists. They cite Exodus 20:4: "Thou shalt not make unto thee any graven image," and a statue is certainly a "graven image"—that is, an image made by human hands. When this verse is thrown at them, most Catholics are stumped for a response. If they were more familiar with Exodus, they could skip to chapter 25 and read the account of the ornamenting of the Ark of the Covenant. The Lord commanded that the Ark, which held the tablets of the Law, be topped by statues of two cherubim. The statues were to be made of gold, and the wings of the cherubim were to be held over the Ark, as though protecting it.

So here we have the Lord, in chapter 20 saying, "Don't make statues," according to Fundamentalists, and in chapter 25 the Lord says, "Make statues." The key to this apparent contradiction is the purpose behind the making of statues. In chapter 20 statues used in idol worship were condemned; in chapter

25 statues used for a proper religious purpose were praised. This brings us to statues in Catholic churches. Fundamentalists see us kneel before statues of Mary and the saints and conclude we're worshiping either the statues as such or at least the saints represented by the statues. We can't blame them entirely for this misconception. Sometimes the misconception is fostered by our side through imprecise language.

The fact that a Catholic kneels before a statue to pray doesn't mean he's praying to the statue. A Fundamentalist may kneel with a Bible in his hand, but no one thinks he's praying to a book. Statues and other "graven images" are used to recall to the mind the person or thing depicted. Just as it's easier to remember one's family by looking at a photograph, so it's easier to remember the lives of the saints (and thus be edified by them) by looking at representations of the saints.

"But you pray to saints, even if you don't pray to their statues," say Fundamentalists. "That means you do worship them. At the least your prayers to saints violate 1 Timothy 2:5, which says 'There is one mediator between God and man, the man Christ Jesus.'"

Prayers to saints, asking them to intercede with God for us, don't violate 1 Timothy 2:5. If they did, then every Christian would stand guilty of violating that verse because every Christian prays for other people. After all, what is a mediator? Merely a go-between. When we pray for others, we act as go-betweens, passing their concerns to God. Fundamentalists regularly ask one another for prayers. They are right to do this because our Lord commanded that we pray for one another.

No Fundamentalist will say to another, "No, I won't pray for you. Pray to God straight!" Instead, he'll say, "I'll gladly pray for you, and please pray for me." In so praying he becomes a mediator. This doesn't violate 1 Timothy 2:5, which is really telling us that our prayers for one another are effectual

20

precisely because Christ is the one mediator. Without his mediation, our prayers would be worthless.

If it's proper to ask imperfect Christians on Earth to pray for us, why should it be improper to ask perfected Christians in heaven to pray for us? Death doesn't separate us from Christ or the Church. In fact, death brings us closer to both. Keep in mind the simile of the vine and the branches. Christ is the vine, and we are the branches. This is a singular vine. When a branch dies, it doesn't break off and fall away. It blossoms. It is perfected.

Through Christ we remain in communion with other Christians on Earth—and with Christians in heaven (and in purgatory). On Earth we can ask for our friends' prayers by calling them on the phone, writing an email, using sign language. The only way we can communicate with the saints is through prayer. How can they hear us? We don't know the mechanics of it, but then we don't know the mechanics of how God hears prayers either. To say he hears prayers because he's omnipotent is no answer. That still doesn't tell us how he does it. To claim that saints can't hear us opens us to the claim that God can't hear us either, and no Fundamentalist believes that.

What seems to be the real problem for Fundamentalists? Why do they get so annoyed with Catholics praying to saints? Ultimately it's because they don't have the Mass. The Mass is the highest form of worship possible—sacrifice. The Protestant Reformers did away with the Mass, so all that Fundamentalists, distant heirs of the Reformers, have to fall back on, as the highest form of worship available to them, is straight prayer. Prayer to saints can be confused with prayer to God, if prayer to God is the best one can do. The result: the worship of God may seem indistinguishable from conversation with saints.

Catholics don't have this problem. Yes, we pray to God, but we also have the Mass, which is radically unlike mere prayer and which honors God alone. It's easier for Catholics to keep their "honoring" compartmentalized. Despite hoary stories to the contrary, there have been almost no Catholics who have confused honoring saints with adoring God. That may be why, when Catholics see Fundamentalists kneeling with the Bible in their hands, they never think the Fundamentalists are worshiping a book. The thought just never occurs to them.

Note to a Seminarian

I hope you haven't fallen into the trap of thinking little or nothing in Scripture is to be taken literally. In fact, nearly everything is, and the parts that aren't, such as allegory, poetry, and parables, are pretty obvious. A grave injustice is done to many seminarians by making them think that Scripture is mainly metaphorical.

The problem with your Fundamentalist friend isn't that he takes parts of Scripture literally, but that he takes parts in isolation and takes other parts metaphorically when he should take them literally. The verses you mention, by themselves, may be susceptible to multiple interpretations, and Fundamentalists choose just one. If the verses were seen not just in immediate context but in relation to verses elsewhere in Scripture, the available interpretations would dwindle, often to only one and often to one Fundamentalists don't take.

A good example of this is the verses referring to the "brethren" of the Lord. In Scripture the word "brethren" is susceptible to two chief meanings: uterine brothers and sisters or close relatives. (A third meaning is used by Fundamentalists in their own churches: any fellow Christian is a "brother" or "sister," which is why the minister refers to "Brother Smith" and "Sister Jones," even though Smith and Jones aren't related by blood.) The Fundamentalist takes these "brethren" verses in the first sense and lets it go at that. If he investigated other verses concerning Mary's perpetual virginity—or alleged lack of it—he would see that "brethren" in the narrow, uterine sense is an interpretation that won't work.

Keep in mind that, to understand the import of a verse, we need to examine not just those around it, the immediate context, but perhaps verses far removed that don't seem to have anything to do with the issue. For instance, in pondering the relation of the "brethren of the Lord" to Mary (were they her sons and daughters or more distant relatives?), we need to be able to stand far enough back to see that, while the sacred writers refer to Jesus as the "son of Mary," never once are these "brethren" referred to as the sons or daughters of Mary. This bifurcation is striking because it is abnormal. Writers tend to keep the same style throughout a work. Why refer to only one child in a family as the son of the mother? Why not refer to all of the children as the sons and daughters of the mother? Why relegate the other children to a status in which they are not ever referred to as Mary's children but only as brothers and sisters of Jesus? It's no answer to say, "Because Jesus is more important than Mary"—which is true, but irrelevant to the issue.

When the Jews referred to "brethren," the use of the term was ambiguous because of the limitations of Hebrew and Aramaic, each being deficient in words for close relations, "brethren" being used instead. My point is that we can't draw any conclusion, one way or the other, about the relation of the "brethren" to Christ if we restrict ourselves to the "brethren" verses. We must act as detectives and see if there are other verses, often far removed from these, that indicate something about Mary's relation to these people. My argument is that there are multiple verses that are incompatible with her being their mother. While no one verse is adequate to prove the matter, all of them taken together provide a high level of confidence, approaching certainty, I think. Beyond that Scripture is silent on the issue. There is no verse that states explicitly that the "brethren" were or were not Mary's children, and we must make do with whatever other evidence we can gather. (I abstract here, of course, from relying on authority, the Church having authority to determine this matter, even if Scripture were to say nothing about it.)

24

I will make one point that you neglect to allude to. You rightly note that James, Joseph, Simon, and Jude are in one verse named as Jesus' "brethren." You ignore that two of them are elsewhere named as the sons of Mary, wife of Cleophas, not of Mary, wife of Joseph. Since they can't have had two biological mothers, they must not be children of Jesus' mother and therefore must not be Jesus' blood brethren. Most Protestant scholars, so far as I can tell, acknowledge that "brethren" is ambiguous and can't be used to settle the issue one way or the other.

I suppose if I had no pre-existing belief in many Christian doctrines I wouldn't come to them solely through a reading of Scripture—and neither would you. At least I know that many people have been unable to do so. The divinity of the Holy Spirit is a doctrine that pops to mind. It's not at all clear from Scripture that the Holy Spirit is of the Godhead. If it were clear, we would not have seen the pneumatomachian heresies of the early centuries. One could argue, I suppose—and people did argue—that the "clear" sense of Scripture is that the Holy Spirit is God's force or influence but is not a Person—or at least not a divine Person. It's the *sola scriptura* advocate who, historically, had a problem with the Holy Spirit verses. Those recognizing Church authority had no problem, because they knew how the verses were to be understood.

Blindness and the Bible-Alone Theory

I was invited to engage in a "written debate" with Dick Knolls, a Protestant controversialist. The subject was authority. The first installment, by Knolls, brought up a number of issues, some of them directly on point, others peripheral but interesting. In my rejoinder I concentrated on a few that seemed to demand immediate comment. Keep in mind that I was writing to a Protestant readership:

I'm grateful for this opportunity to respond to Dick Knolls' essay on *sola scriptura*. He has stated the traditional Protestant position in forceful language, and he won't object, I'm sure, if I write frankly about the Catholic position. This exchange is intended to help you obtain a rounded view of the issue of authority, and often the best way to obtain such a view is to read opposing arguments.

First, a few preliminary comments. Twice Mr. Knolls refers to the "blind followers" of the Catholic Church. He says that, "through the trickery of men" and "by craftiness in deceitful scheming," the leaders of the Catholic Church have bamboozled its members into accepting its beliefs. Since I'm a Catholic layman and not a cleric, I suppose I'm classed as one of the blind, one of the bamboozled.

I don't think this notion of Catholic laymen being tricked into being Catholics holds water, and not just because I don't like being classed with the intellectually blind. A Catholic can point to any number of clear-headed converts to his faith who are anything but blind (unless you define blindness as being the same as being a Catholic, but that's special pleading). The very fact that these people have entered the Catholic Church argues against the idea that Catholics are tricked into submission. Consider three contemporary examples.

Jean-Marie Lustiger, who died in 2007, was the cardinal archbishop of Paris. He was a convert from Judaism and was a man whose family was persecuted by the Nazis and whose conversion to Christianity cost him dearly. (His family strongly opposed his becoming a Christian.) He was a man with a sharp mind—hardly the kind who would be bamboozled.

Or consider the late Sheldon Vanauken. You might know him as the author of *A Severe Mercy,* the best-selling book about the love affair he had with his wife, who died young. Vanauken grew up a pagan (his term), but became a Protestant under the tutelage of C. S. Lewis. Late in life he converted to Catholicism. If you read his books, which are beautifully written, you will see they aren't the kinds of things that come from the pen of a man who can be led around by the nose.

As my third example, look at Thomas Howard. He was a highly-respected Evangelical leader and taught at Gordon College. His book *Evangelical is Not Enough,* written while he was a Protestant, is a plea for a more liturgical Evangelicalism. He too converted to Catholicism, seeing it as his real home. (He then lost his job at Gordon College.) Howard isn't the sort of man that can be tricked by a few rascally priests either.

I note this blindness issue because I want to impress upon you that we Catholics aren't all dolts—sure, some of us are, but some Protestants are too—and we hold our faith not because we're under the thumb of rapacious clerics but because we believe it to be true. We're people who are not ignorant about secular things; you will find many of us skilled in our occupations and in things of common knowledge. Is it likely, then, that we have become and remain Catholics for no good reason at all?

(Just as there is this "priestcraft" argument, which is given to explain why people are Catholics, there is an analogous argument, usually advanced by secularists, that people become Fundamentalists because they're ignorant, poor, and lonely. This is a caricature, as can be demonstrated easily by pointing to the many Fundamentalists who are intelligent, not poor, and not lonely.)

Often I have spoken before audiences partly or largely Protestant; sometimes the speaking has been in the form of debates. When the evening begins, many of the Protestants are of the opinion that nothing can be said in favor of the Catholic faith. After all, they've never heard the Catholic side. By the time the debate concludes, they haven't become Catholics, but many of them have come to realize that Catholics have rational things to say and that there exist sensible, even if not (to them) convincing, arguments in favor of Catholicism.

Another point. Arguments deserve to be evaluated on their own merits. We don't answer an argument by saying no one but a fool would hold such a position. That isn't an answer at all. When we engage in argumentation (which, by the way, is an honorable thing to do—it needn't imply yelling at each other), we should make sure we begin at the beginning. We have to get our principles straight, and we should be clear about what we take as presuppositions.

Mr. Knolls (to return, finally, to his essay) classifies Catholicism as a cult. I won't go into why I don't think this kind of labeling is helpful. I want to direct your attention to his reasoning here. He says Catholicism "adds supplementary authorities alongside the Scripture, as do the cults. It is not *sola scriptura* for Rome but Scripture ... and traditions with both subject to the interpretation which the teaching magisterium of Rome alone can give it." Note the syllogism: (1) A cult is a religion not based on *sola scriptura.* (2) Catholicism is not based on *sola scriptura.* (3) Thus, Catholicism is a cult. Do you see what is unexamined here? Step back from the definition of a cult, and what presupposition do you see? That Christianity is based on *sola scriptura.* But this shouldn't be a presupposition. This is something that needs to be demonstrated.

The Catholic position is that *sola scriptura* is non-scriptural. Let me put in plainly: the Bible nowhere states that the Bible alone is the sole rule of faith. The principle of *sola scriptura* is not found in Christian writings prior to the Reformation, with the exception of a very few, isolated writings that historians are unable to connect with one another and that were penned by people who did not hold what today would be called Protestant beliefs. The principle of *sola scriptura* is, in fact, an "invention," to use the word some Protestant controversialists employ to describe peculiarly Catholic beliefs.

When I make this sort of comment at a debate—when I say the Bible doesn't support *sola scriptura*—I leave the discussion open-ended. I don't give a full proof immediately. I hold off because I'm sure some Protestant listener will offer a rebuttal during the question period. He'll refer to 2 Timothy 3:16–17. The questioner will ask, "Doesn't this prove our position?"

"Not at all," I reply. Here's why. First, let's not prejudge the verse. It's been used so long as a proof of *sola scriptura* that folks no longer ask, "Does it really prove this doctrine?" Look at what's actually happening. Paul is instructing Timothy. He has just told him to hold fast to the doctrine that has been handed on to him. Then he says that everything in Scripture has been divinely inspired, and what is in Scripture has various uses. It can be used to instruct, to expose errors, to correct faults, and to educate in holy living.

No Catholic denies any of this. But is the apostle saying what Mr. Knolls claims? He asks, "Can any other conclusion be validly drawn from this text except that Scripture *alone* is all that a child of God needs for instruction ...?" Not only is my answer "Yes," but it is that the text doesn't support *sola scriptura* in the least.

Look at the words carefully. There is no mention about Scripture being sufficient, on its own. Paul says Scripture is "profitable" for these various ends. That doesn't mean some other thing, or other things, might not be profitable also. Consider an analogy. We might say that water is profitable for bodily health—that it can help us achieve it—but that isn't the same thing as saying water is all we need to remain healthy. We need solid food and exercise too. Paul says Scripture is profitable, but he doesn't say it's the only thing that is profitable. Profitableness doesn't equal sufficiency.

That's one way to disprove *sola scriptura.* Here's another. Presume this passage did prove *solve scriptura.* If it did, it would prove too much. Let me explain that. If 2 Timothy 3:16–17 proves Scripture alone is all that's needed, it must prove that Timothy had on hand all he needed. What did he have on hand? Not the Bible as we know it. The New Testament wasn't written then, and if any New Testament books were in existence when Paul instructed Timothy, they weren't yet accepted by Christians as part of the canon of the Bible. For Timothy, Scripture was what we call the Old Testament and that alone.

If Paul's comment really implies *sola scriptura,* then it implies that the Old Testament alone is sufficient as a rule of faith. Does any Christian believe that? Of course not. I'm not trying to be tricky here, the way Mr. Knolls thinks Catholic priests are tricky. I'm not trying to fool anyone, and I'm not even presenting a new argument. This argument, about proving too much, is not original with me. I borrowed it from John Henry Newman—hardly a slouch in intellectual matters.

Newman, who had had a born-again experience at age fifteen, was a convert from Evangelicalism to Catholicism.

Why is 2 Timothy 3:16–17 always brought up when the issue is *sola scriptura?* Force of habit, perhaps. It's always been used when one Protestant explains to another why *sola scriptura* must be true, but the Protestant to whom the explanation is made accepts *sola scriptura* anyway. He isn't inclined to test alleged proofs, to see if they really prove what they purport to prove. He doesn't take the text at arm's length and look at it from various angles.

Four Inadequate Reasons—and a Fifth

There are four ways to prove the Bible is true, says John E. MacArthur, Jr., in *Why Believe the Bible*. Unfortunately for him, not one of the reasons he gives is solid. Each, in its own way, may be convincing—that is, each of his arguments may convince someone. But bad arguments convince people all the time. The problem with bad arguments is that folks who see them today may see through them tomorrow, and then they have nothing to fall back on. Far better, surely, to be given a solid argument to begin with. But that's getting ahead of the story.

MacArthur is pastor of Grace Community Church in Panorama City, California, "where he ministers to several thousand each week." His book seems to be intended for the new Evangelical—not for the New Evangelical, a term which sometimes means an Evangelical who has lost his faith, but for the new Christian of an Evangelical bent. Strict Fundamentalists may decline to read *Why Believe the Bible* because its scriptural quotations are taken mainly from the New International Version instead of the King James Version, but, if they turn the cover, they'll find little to object to. What MacArthur says can be accepted by most "conservative" Protestants.

In the second chapter MacArthur asks, "What can you say when someone wants you to prove the Bible is true?" You can begin, he says, with the argument from personal experience. "I believe the Bible is true because it gives me the experience that it claims it will give me. For example, the Bible says that God will forgive my sins. I believe that. I accepted God's forgiveness and it happened. How do I know? I have a sense of freedom from guilt."

Let's pause here. Weaknesses are popping up already. MacArthur says the truth of the Bible is evident "because it gives me the experience that it claims it will give me." If the back cover of a horror story claims the book will give you the willies and then delivers on its promise, is the story somehow true? Hardly. If a chemistry text claims to make you a better chemist than all your neighbors and then does so, does that imply everything it has taught you is correct chemistry—or have you, perhaps, been fed truth and error, but not told which is which? If a book does what it claims, does that prove it's true? Of course not.

Okay, so this may be reading more into MacArthur's words than they deserve. After all, he does qualify his comment with an example. The Bible says his sins will be forgiven. He has "a sense of freedom from guilt," implying his sins indeed have been forgiven. Therefore the Bible is true. Sounds good, eh? The problem is that it's a lousy syllogism. The secular humanist, absorbing each nuance of Humanist Manifesto II, declares that he now enjoys "a sense of freedom from guilt." Is the Manifesto therefore true? If so, the Bible can't be, and vice versa. Feeling guilt-free might mean your sins have been forgiven, but it might mean your conscience is sleeping or is malformed.

Let's continue with MacArthur's first argument. He says "the Bible really changes lives. Millions of people—from great heads of state to brilliant educators and scientists, from philosophers and writers to generals and historians—could all testify about how the Bible has changed their lives. As somebody has said, 'A Bible that is falling apart usually belongs to someone who isn't.' Millions of people are living proof that the Bible can put lives together and keep them that way."

Yes, but not just the Bible. The devout Muslim can point to the way the Koran changed his life, and the Mormon can argue that he is a better person since obeying the strictures of the Book of Mormon. Even non-believers can point to books that improved them. Consider the account Sheldon Vanauken gave in *A Severe Mercy* of his pagan (his term) days, when good poetry and great literature manifestly improved him. Are we to conclude, then, that Eliot and Shakespeare are inspired? Inspiring, certainly, but that's a different thing. Although reform in lives is a sign that the Bible is true, it isn't itself a proof.

"A stronger argument," says MacArthur, "comes from science. Although the Bible is not a science book the descriptions referring to scientific processes are accurate." He refers to the hydrological cycle: rain falls, the runoff gathers into streams, the streams coalesce into rivers, the rivers pour into the oceans, and from the oceans water evaporates and forms clouds, from which rain again falls. "The hydrological cycle is a discovery of fairly modern times," claims MacArthur, "but the Bible speaks of it in Isaiah 55:10: 'As the rain and the snow come down from heaven, and do not return to it without watering the earth.'" MacArthur might be disappointed to discover similar comments in ancient Roman and Greek literature. After all, the observation verges on the pedestrian, and Isaiah was not expounding meteorological theories.

But MacArthur has a better scientific illustration. "Geologists speak of a state called isostasy. ... Basically the idea behind isostasy is that equal weights are necessary to support equal weights. Land mass must be balanced equally by water mass. In order for the earth to remain stable as it spins in orbit, it must be in perfect balance. But again, the scientists haven't discovered anything that is significantly new or beyond the Bible. The prophet Isaiah also wrote that God 'measured the waters in the hollow of his hand' and that he 'weighed the mountains on the scales and the hills in a balance' (Isa. 40:12)."

One problem here is that MacArthur misunderstands isostasy—one may presume he is unfamiliar with the theories of Archdeacon Pratt and G. B. Airy, who in 1855 wrote about what later became known as isostasy—but you don't need to know anything about it to see that Isaiah's poetic reference to God as Creator can't be reinterpreted to be a veiled reference to a modern geological theory.

"You can find many other examples of how the Bible matches up with discoveries of modern science," notes MacArthur. Sure, but it would be hard to point to a book of wide scope that did not have correlations with modern science. "Of course," writes MacArthur, "the precise technological language is not there, and for good reason. God wrote the Bible for men of all ages and while his word never contradicts science, it also never gets trapped into describing some precise scientific theory that becomes outdated in a few years, decades, or centuries." That's true, but it's also true that "precise technological language is not there" because the Bible wasn't written to teach science in the first place.

To the third proof. "A third significant area that has continued to prove the Bible's accuracy is archaeology. ... Archaeology confirms the authority of the Bible" and "helps us see clearly that our Christian faith rests on facts (actual events) not myths or stories." He is referring here mainly to things in the Old Testament, and he's quite right. Scoffers are finding themselves holding their tongues now. Once they declared the history given in the Bible to be imaginative but inaccurate, but archaeological investigations keep confirming elements of that history.

So, MacArthur is right on that point, but all it means is that the Bible is being shown to contain accurate historical accounts. That doesn't prove the religion enshrined in the Bible is true. Edward Gibbon's *History of the Decline and Fall of the*

Roman Empire may be pointed to as getting Roman history right, but are we to conclude that his unflattering comments about Christianity are to be taken as gospel truth? A book's historical accuracy is no guarantee that its religious views are right.

"Perhaps the strongest objective argument for the validity of Scripture comes from fulfilled Bible prophecy." MacArthur cites mathematician Peter W. Stoner, who "asked 600 of his students to apply the principle of probability to the biblical prophecy of the destruction of Tyre (see Ezek. 26:3–16), which claims seven definite events." These events were that Nebuchadnezzar would capture the city, that "other nations would help fulfill the prophecy," that Tyre would be leveled, that "the city would become a place where fishermen spread their nets," that "Tyre's stones and timbers would be laid in the sea," that inhabitants of other cities would worry for their own safety because of Tyre's fall, and that "the old city of Tyre would never be rebuilt.

"Using the principle of probability in a conservative manner," says MacArthur, "the students estimated the chances of all seven events occurring as described at one in 400 million, yet all seven did occur. Stoner's students did a similar study on the prophecy that predicted the fall of Babylon (see Isa. 13:19). They estimated the chances of the Babylon prophecies occurring at one in 100 billion, but everything stated did come to pass. Biblical prophecy declares the events of the future with accuracy which is beyond the capability of human wisdom or anticipation. Despite astronomical odds, hundreds of biblical prophecies have come true, and they make the most objective argument for the Bible's authority."

Well, if the mathematical argument is the most objective one there is, the Bible is in trouble. First of all, the argument is ill defined. How did the students come up with those numbers?

If you assume an event is as likely to occur as not to occur—that is, that it has a one in two chance of occurring—then the odds that seven events will occur, as in the first example, are one in 128, not one in 400 million. To get one in 400 million you must assume each of the seven events, considered by itself, is very unlikely to occur. Here's another wrinkle. If Nebuchadnezzar captured Tyre and leveled it, you'd expect stones and timbers to end up in the sea (Tyre being a seaport after all) and that fishermen would use deserted pavements for spreading their nets. You'd certainly conclude neighboring people would be scared out of their wits. And so on.

In other words, if a city is captured, certain other events are almost sure to happen. Some naturally go together: if A happens, B and C are implied. So instead of seven independent events, for mathematical purposes you might be talking of three or four, and you might have to conclude that the likelihood of Nebuchadnezzar capturing Tyre was only one in 100 million, if you want to end up with overall odds of one in 400 million. But could it have been that unlikely that Nebuchadnezzar, the most powerful king of the region, would take Tyre?

These comments are not meant to question the fact of biblical prophecy—far from it. They're meant to show that applying mathematical formulas to the fulfillment of prophecies is almost valueless. Presumably, MacArthur would not trot out this stuff if the numbers weren't so impressive. If Stoner's students had concluded the odds of the prophecies coming true had been one in ten, say, instead of one in 400 million or one in 100 billion, MacArthur might have realized that his argument implied a one in ten chance of the Bible being untrue, and those are uncomfortably high odds in so important a matter. No, this probability business is just too fluid for any satisfying proof to come from it.

Besides, there's a much greater problem attached to it. Even if the numbers MacArthur cites were accurate, and even if they constituted proof of inspiration, the most they would prove would be the inspiration of the particular biblical books in which the prophecies appear. They wouldn't prove the inspiration of the Bible as a whole. Although prophecies (taken in the sense of predictions of future events) argue in favor of the faith, they don't argue in favor of the inspiration of the Bible as a whole. How can prophecies in Isaiah prove the inspiration, the truth, of the Book of Proverbs, or Ecclesiastes, or the Song of Songs (which, for example, contains no prophecies of its own)? They can't, of course. As soon as someone convinced by MacArthur's proofs of the truth of the Bible realizes that, he will become unconvinced. A second-rate argument, when seen through, may be worse than no argument at all. People are likely to throw up their hands in despair.

MacArthur seems to sense this, and at the end of the chapter he falls into a kind of despair himself, asserting that there are no proofs. "Actually there is only one argument that can prove to us that the Bible is true and authoritative for our lives: the work of the Holy Spirit in our hearts and minds. ... While the Christian can marshal good arguments from personal experience, science, archaeology, and prophecy, he cannot finally 'prove' the Bible is true and authoritative. Still, he knows the Bible is true because of his resident truth-teacher—the Holy Spirit. The Holy Spirit is the only one who can prove God's Word is true and he does this as he works in the heart and mind of the Christian whom he indwells."

In other words, the four arguments MacArthur gives are not enough. They do not prove what he, inconsistently, claims they prove. MacArthur's Christian must fall back on what Arnold Lunn, one of the twentieth century's foremost lay Catholic apologists, termed "fif," which stands for "funny internal feeling": the Bible is true because I feel it to be true. This is mere subjectivism, and it is no argument at all to anyone but the convinced Christian. Even then it is a weak argument. After all, the convinced Muslim enjoys "fif" also, but with respect to the Koran, and the atheist may feel "fiffy" when he reads Nietzsche or Feuerbach, and the glutton may conclude the only true words are found in menus, because he goes all aflutter when he enters a restaurant.

A final comment. MacArthur ends by saying the Christian "cannot finally 'prove' the Bible is true." Wrong. We can establish the Bible's truth through the application of reason. We don't have to fall back on some variant of fideism, the belief that human reason is incapable of attaining any truth apart from revelation. The truth of the Bible, which follows from its inspiration, can be established through reason. Catholics can come up with solid reasons for accepting the Bible. We don't have to rely on "fif."

Looking Foolish

From Islington, Ontario, I received a letter which sheds light on the public perception of Catholics. It is from a self-described Fundamentalist who volunteered to see if he can arrange a debate between me and a prominent exponent of his position. Although anxious to set up a debate, my correspondent was concerned about what might happen to me if I found myself on a platform with his champion. "It does not seem fair that one like yourself, who is a layman of the Roman Catholic Church, should be made to look foolish in going into a debate with someone who is one of the foremost authorities on Church history and the Roman Catholic religion."

The writer might have been quite right in saying I would be made to look foolish in such a debate—my debate opponent might, after all, be a splendid orator, and, in a public talk, that could more than balance out the inherent weaknesses of his religious position. What's more, I've looked foolish when speaking in public before, so it can happen again. I told the writer I appreciated his concern, yet I found his comment more revealing than he might have suspected.

He didn't know me, and yet was convinced I wouldn't have a prayer against his hero. It isn't that he doubted my argumentative skills from having seen me in action. He didn't base his comment on long hours spent watching me put my foot in my mouth, since he knew nothing of me beyond what I have written in various places. To him I was little more than an uppity Catholic willing to put his head on the block. I could be the best-educated, best-speaking Catholic around, but it would make no difference because his attitude had nothing to do with me as an individual, which is why I took no offence.

No matter how well trained or natively intelligent a Catholic might be, it is an axiom for this fellow that a Catholic can't hold his own in a public discussion. He doesn't think this merely because, as a Fundamentalist, he finds the Catholic position ludicrous. There is something more. It is the belief that Catholics can't think, precisely because they're Catholics. No matter how fine their minds before, no matter how extensive their oratorical powers, in becoming Catholics they forfeit unfettered thought and the ability to argue as they once could; they submit to a tyranny and in doing so give up their intellectual freedom. If they are "cradle Catholics," then they always have been hopeless.

It is not simply that Catholicism is wrong, that Catholics follow mistaken beliefs. It is worse than that. Like so many others, my correspondent sees Catholicism as a positive hindrance to thought. He thinks it shuts off the mind from anything other than what an authoritarian Church tells its members to think. No matter how smart a man might otherwise be, he does himself in, he commits intellectual suicide, by following Rome. People in other churches or no church are merely mistaken, but Catholics are mentally lost.

You might say this is just the anti-Catholic attitude common among Protestants years ago. No, it is more than that. It is not opposition to the Catholic religion in the sense one opposes some ideology because it is a mixture of error and truth, nor is it an attitude restricted to old-line Protestants. In fact, it is the (usually unacknowledged) attitude of many Americans, Fundamentalists, irreligious skeptics, and people in between.

It is associated with Fundamentalists because they happen to be guileless enough to mention it. To them Catholics' inability to think is a simple fact and seems to be nothing at which Catholics should take offence, just as a paraplegic should take no offence in being told he won't win the footrace. These are just facts of life. The man's comment is just the public acknowledgement of a disability—in this case, a mental disability.

His attitude arises from the notion that submission to an ecclesiastical authority stultifies the mind. In submitting, one gives up intellectual freedom for emotional security. Of course, the problem is really a failure of the imagination on the part of people who hold this man's position. They are unable to see that through submission to truth one becomes free to go after still more truth.

G. K. Chesterton put it in terms of dogmas. When accused of being dogmatic, he joyfully acknowledged that the word applied, but not in the usual sense of being close-minded. Just the opposite, in fact. Our intellectual task in life, he said, is to seize upon dogmas—in whatever field—and stuff them in a bag. The more we get, the more we are able to get. In religion, if we can rely on the infallible authority of the Church, so much the better. It gives us a leg up in the most important subject of all, our final destiny. Instead of limiting what we can do (which at first glance it might seem to), this reliance on authority gives us a solid base from which to work.

Hairballs

I was debating a former priest who headed a ministry that tried to lure Catholics into "real" Christianity. In the question period a young woman raised her hand. She looked angry and, turning to me, said, "My grandmother lives in Mexico. She is a pious Catholic. She goes to Mass every week and prays the rosary every day. Under her bed she keeps a glass jar with a hairball in it, and she worships the hairball. Why does your church promote such idolatry?"

I explained to her that worshiping hairballs is no part of Catholic practice, and she seemed to accept the plea of innocence. She seemed to recognize that we shouldn't be blamed for something we would condemn, if we only knew about it. Then questions turned to real, not imagined, Catholic practices, ones that Fundamentalists find repellent. We might call these the "smells and bells" of Catholicism. These are activities that mark Catholics as Catholics, things we do that make us stand out.

On the whole, Fundamentalists dislike peculiarly Catholic customs because they think they're non-scriptural, even anti-scriptural. This attitude can be overcome, but it takes patience. First, we must explain what we mean by a particular practice (many Fundamentalists don't know, say, what the sign of the cross is—they don't know the motions, and they don't know the words). Then we must explain why we do these things (because they bring to mind our Lord's redemptive work, for instance). Third, we must question Fundamentalists closely to see if they harbor some unusual misunderstanding of our practices. Many of them do.

We need to impress upon them that Catholicism is a sacramental religion. Sacraments are visible signs of God's grace.

They are actions that not only signify the transmittal of grace to us but really do transmit grace. They are a natural consequence of the Incarnation: God took on flesh (matter) to save us, and he left behind actions that use matter (such as water, oil, and wine) to continue to give us his saving grace. Unlike Catholicism, Fundamentalism is not a sacramental religion. It's one thing, Fundamentalists say, for God to take flesh and to use material things during his sojourn on Earth. It's something else for him to set up a Church that encourages the continued use of material things. God is too great, too "wholly other," to use matter as a vehicle of grace.

Aside from the seven sacraments, Catholics have sacramentals, and in some ways sacramentals are more off-putting to Fundamentalists than are the seven sacraments themselves. After all, even Fundamentalists have the "ordinances" of baptism and the Lord's Supper, even though they don't think these "ordinances" do what our sacraments of baptism and the Eucharist do. But Fundamentalists have nothing like sacramentals, or so they think.

The Code of Canon Law explains that "sacramentals are sacred signs by which spiritual effects are signified and are obtained by the intercession of the Church" (can. 1166). They aren't the ordinary means of grace established by Christ—that is, they aren't sacraments as such—but they are related to sacraments. With sacramentals we consecrate our daily lives and keep thoughts of God ever in our minds. There are seven sacraments but countless sacramentals. Any action or thing put to a sacred purpose may be considered a sacramental.

Fundamentalists use sacramentals, but they don't realize it. Consider the Protestant wedding ceremony. The bride wears white and, perhaps, a veil. She carries a bouquet. She and the groom exchange vows and rings. Each action and thing has a religious significance: purity in the white garments, fidelity in

44

the vows, for instance. Each is a sign of the holiness of matrimony. Each is a sacramental (if the word is used in a wide sense). If spoken to gently, Fundamentalists can come to accept the fact that they too use sacramentals, even if they dislike the word. They are especially uncomfortable, though, when told many of these sacramentals originated in pagan religions. After all, the standard Fundamentalist charge against Catholicism is that its distinctive customs and beliefs are of pagan origin. Fundamentalists don't want to admit that they too have borrowed from paganism, but that is exactly what they have done. After all, their churches are offshoots of offshoots from the Catholic Church, even if they won't admit the fact. (Fundamentalists believe their brand of Christianity goes straight back to New Testament times. It actually goes back only to the nineteenth century.)

Let's look at a few Catholic practices that irk Fundamentalists.

Genuflecting. When they pass the Blessed Sacrament, Catholics go down on one knee to honor the Real Presence. This posture of subservience makes perfect sense since Christ is present in the tabernacle. Fundamentalists don't believe he's there, of course (they believe instead in a Real Absence), but they can be made to acknowledge the sensibleness of genuflecting through analogy. Ask them to imagine themselves at Buckingham Palace, at an audience with the Queen of England. She enters the room and walks up to a woman. Under court protocol, what is the woman supposed to do? She is supposed to curtsy as a sign of respect for the Queen.

Another analogy. A soldier meets an officer on the street. What does the soldier do? He salutes. Again, a sign of respect and an acknowledgement of a superior. Who is more superior to us than God? Which Fundamentalist, transported back to first century Palestine, would not throw himself prostrate at the sight of Jesus? If that would be proper, then why not genuflect where Jesus is sacramentally present?

Similarly, at Mass we stand when the Gospel is read, out of respect for the very words of Jesus, and we sit to listen attentively to the other scriptural readings. At the consecration we kneel, kneeling being the posture of adoration. What we are doing is praying with our bodies, not just with our minds, and praying that way makes sense for a creature composed of both body and soul.

Sign of the cross. Every Fundamentalist knows Catholics cross themselves when praying in church, when hiding in foxholes, and when waiting in the on-deck circle to bat. They don't, as a rule, know that Eastern Orthodox Christians also cross themselves (although they do it "backwards"), so they think the sign of the cross is something that immediately distinguishes Catholics from "real" Christians.

They don't know that "real" Christians began making the sign of the cross at a very early date. The theologian Tertullian, writing in 211, recorded the practice. True, the practice is not mentioned in the New Testament, but neither are peculiarly Fundamentalist practices such as the altar call, in which people march to the front of a church to announce publicly that, because of the preaching, they have just decided to "make a commitment to Christ." The sign of the cross signifies two things at once: our redemption through the death of Jesus on the cross and the Trinity as the central truth of Christianity. When we make the sign we trace the cross on ourselves, and we recite the holy invocation: "In the name of the Father, and of the Son, and of the Holy Spirit."

Incense. Not used as often in our liturgies as it once was, incense symbolizes the pleasant odor of Christian virtue and our prayers rising to God. It is the first half of the "smells and bells." Most Fundamentalists think only Catholics use incense, but incense is not peculiar to Catholics. The ancient Jews used it. Incense accompanied prayers at the Temple (Luke 1:10), and one of the gifts given to the Christ Child by the Magi was frankincense (Matt. 2:11). But all that was before Christianity began, say Fundamentalists. Maybe so, but the book of Revelation deals with what happens *afterwards*, and there we find that "the smoke of the incense rose with the prayers of the saints from the hand of the angel before God" (Rev. 8:4). If there's incense in heaven, why not in churches here below?

Bells. Our church towers commonly have bells, often consisting of large sets, known as carillons, that can be rung from a keyboard. Bells have been used for centuries to call people to Mass and to sanctify certain times of the day—for instance, it once was the custom, in Catholic countries, to ring church bells at noon so workers in the fields could pause and recite the Angelus. During Mass handbells are rung at the consecration, partly to focus our attention, partly to mimic the hosannahs of the heavenly choirs.

Fundamentalists disapprove of bells being used in Christian worship. Why they disapprove isn't very clear. Some say bells are of pagan origin and thus should be forbidden, but pagans also sang hymns, and no Fundamentalist thinks Christian hymns should be forbidden. Other Fundamentalists are more straightforward: they don't like bells because bells are identified in their minds with the Catholic Church. Of course, Protestant churches often have bell towers, but that's overlooked by these Fundamentalists. For them opposition to bells is purely a matter of prejudice.

Rosary. The usual complaint about the rosary is that it violates Matthew 6:7, which reads this way in the King James Version: "But when ye pray, use not vain repetitions, as the heathen do." "See," say Fundamentalists, "you Catholics repeat prayers, and Jesus told us not to do that!" Did he really?

Then how does one account for what happened in the garden of Gethsemane? There Jesus prayed the same prayer three times—that is, he repeated the prayer. Did he violate his own injunction? Was he a hypocrite? No, that's impossible, which means Fundamentalists are wrong when they claim Jesus condemned repeated prayers. Read Matthew 6:7 again. The operative word isn't "repetitions." It's "vain." Jesus condemned vain prayers, such as those to non-existent pagan gods.

What's more, the rosary is an intensely biblical prayer. It contains not just the Our Father, which Jesus himself taught us, but also the Hail Mary, which is built of verses lifted from the Bible: "Hail, full of grace, the Lord is with thee" (Luke 1:28) and "blessed art thou among women, and blessed is the fruit of thy womb" (Luke 1:42). The meditations associated with each decade—Catholics call them "mysteries"—are also straight out of the Bible, but most Fundamentalists don't realize this. They think Catholics rattle off Hail Marys without giving a thought to what they're doing. But when we pray the rosary we meditate on incidents in salvation history, such as the Annunciation, the Nativity, the Crucifixion, and the Resurrection.

Priestly vestments. Uniforms single out people engaged in particular functions. The soldier's uniform tells us his vocation, the police officer's uniform helps him be identified by someone looking for help, and the Roman collar marks the priest. Vestments—a sacred "uniform"—are used at Mass. In this the Church follows the example of the Old Testament liturgy, in which priests were dressed in special clothes (Ex. 40:13–14, Lev. 8:7–9), and of the New Testament, which tells us that John the Baptist "wore clothing made of camel's hair and had a leather belt around his waist" (Matt. 3:4).

Holy water. Water covers most of the Earth, and it is absolutely necessary for life. No wonder this marvelous liquid is used in sacraments and sacramentals. Sacred uses of water are found throughout the Old Testament: the saving of the Israelites by the parting of the Red Sea (Ex. 14:15–22), the miraculous flow from the rock touched by Moses' staff (Ex. 17:6–7), the crossing of the Jordan into the Promised Land (Jos. 3:14–17), Ezekiel's vision of life-giving water flowing from the Temple (Ezek. 47:1–12). In the New Testament we find the baptism of Jesus (Matt. 3:13–17), the healing water of the pool of Bethesda (John 5:1–9), and the water brought forth from Jesus' side by the spear thrust (John 19:34). We're told by our Lord that to enter the kingdom of God we must be born of water and the Holy Spirit (John 3:5). With all these holy uses of water, is it any wonder the Church promotes the use of holy water? We find it at baptisms, in exorcisms, and in the stoups at the door of churches. With it we bless ourselves (there's the sign of the cross again!), not because the water itself has any special powers—it's ordinary tap water with a pinch of salt added—but because its pious use brings to mind the truths of our faith.

If we take the time, we can help Fundamentalists see that "smells and bells" flow naturally from the Incarnation, but it takes work. Many Fundamentalists are what might be termed hereditary anti-Catholics. If something is Catholic, they don't like it, period. They operate from prejudice, not from dispassionate thinking. Yet even the most prejudiced can come to appreciate the sensibleness of sacramentals if they have sacramentals explained to them by a patient Catholic.

How Evangelicals Handle Cults

If you visit a "Christian" book store—that is, one with books appealing mainly to Evangelicals and Fundamentalists—you'll find several shelves given over to works debunking the cults. When conservative Protestants use the word "cult," they don't have in mind such things as the cult of a saint. They mean instead religions, more or less removed in appearance from Christianity, that provide believers not just a set of doctrines but social and emotional support that is so intense that the believers are disinclined to question the doctrines. Some Fundamentalists go so far as to claim Catholicism is a cult, but this is a minority viewpoint. Most Fundamentalists say Catholicism isn't a cult—it's just wrong.

But this isn't about attitudes toward Catholicism. It's about what Catholics can learn from Protestants who write against cults. Consider one writer in particular, Anthony A. Hoekema, a professor of systematic theology, a Calvinist, and the author of *The Four Major Cults*. The religions Hoekema examines are Mormonism, Seventh-day Adventism, Christian Science, and the Jehovah's Witnesses. The final chapter of his book is called "Approaching the Cultist," and it's his recommendations that are examined here.

(By the way: I reproduce Hoekema's use of the words "cult" and "cultist," even though their use might strike Catholics as sometimes uncharitable, sometimes improper. I use them merely out of convenience, so my language parallels Hoekema's. Normally I don't use the terms when discussing what William Whalen, a Catholic writer, terms "minority religions." They have a pejorative ring to them, and their use encourages finger-pointing. All some people need to do, to write off a religion, is to label it a cult. Catholics have been at the receiving end of such labeling and should be careful about taking up such loaded words.)

The first subsection of Hoekema's last chapter is about "difficulties." The problems are several, he says. "To begin with, the cultist is not a religiously indifferent person; he is 'deeply religious' to the point of fanaticism. Having rejected historic Christianity, he can be counted on to be antagonistic to the testimony of a Christian believer." What's more, "the cultist firmly believes he has found the truth, and hence he considers the message of historic Christianity to be inferior to the doctrines he has obtained through 'special revelation' or through some inspired channel of truth." The cultist is a victim of a "kind of mass delusion of grandeur, coupled with a great deal of pride." He has had "to endure considerable ridicule from his kith and kin since joining the cult and is even now sacrificing much of his time and effort in making propaganda for the group. Hence it is not going to be easy to induce him to leave the cult."

Hoekema points out, rightly, that "the mere reading of a pamphlet or brochure on a particular cult does not qualify one for conducting a thoroughgoing, polemic against the cult." (The same can be said about those who base their opposition to Catholicism on "the mere reading of a pamphlet or brochure.") To speak with a cultist intelligently, one must be well-grounded in the cult's particular doctrines and in Scripture, says Hoekema.

He refers to a woman who had been a Jehovah's Witness. Going door to door, she "encountered three types of responses. Some slammed doors in her face. These people made her feel good, since their action was construed as persecution for the sake of her faith. A second group of people argued heatedly and belligerently. These only strengthened her convictions, since she had ready answers for their arguments. A third group

51

gave her a personal testimony of their faith in Christ. These, so she said, made the most lasting impression on her; when she went to bed at night, she would think about these people and reflect on what they had said. Surely every true believer ought to be able to give this kind of testimony." And a few true believers should do more, he says. They should make a concerted study of a cult in order to give a Christian response to it.

Before moving on, notice, for a moment, what this woman *didn't* report. She didn't report a fourth group: people who argued with her coolly and charitably. The only arguments she got were heated and belligerent. However important personal testimony is, it isn't enough. We need to use our brains, not just our hearts. (But keep in mind that Catholics, too often trained to think intellectual banter is enough to effect a conversion, often underestimate the power of a personal testimony.) If this woman had encountered a Catholic who not only could testify to what his faith had done for him but one who could explain what the Church really teaches, she might have come all the way to the fullness of Christian faith that is found at Rome.

Hoekema says that the Christian evangelist—he has in mind conservative Protestants, of course—must approach the cultist as a "total person." He means that one shouldn't see the cultist "just as someone whose doctrines need to be refuted but as someone whom we love, about whom we are concerned in the totality of his life. We should therefore try to find out, if we can, why he joined this cult. Did he previously belong to a church? If so, why did he leave it? What shortcomings did he find in it? In what way did the church fail to satisfy his needs? What benefits is he deriving from membership in the group to which he now belongs? What does this group do for him that the church failed to do?"

Much of the attraction of the cults, says Hoekema, is at the social, rather than the doctrinal, level, but he doesn't forget that a person wouldn't stay in a cult if he didn't accept its beliefs. You can do without emotional support, at least for a while; you can't do without intellectual support. When you cease to believe what the cult teaches, you jump ship, no matter how friendly your fellow cultists might be.

Hoekema then comes up with the Big Question: "Right at this point the cultist should be asked, Do you have complete assurance of salvation?" Unlike many Evangelicals and Fundamentalists (but by no means all), the Jehovah's Witness, the Mormon, and the Seventh-day Adventist (and the Catholic, for that matter), will say, No. "Over against this uncertainty we must place the granite certainty of the Christian faith," says Hoekema. He takes as a given that one can have an absolute assurance of salvation, and he doesn't seem to realize that this is, historically, a novel position. It can be traced no further back than the Reformation. It is not the ancient Christian— which is to say, Catholic—position. Here, as elsewhere, Hoekema offers a second-best approach to the cultist. He can't offer anything more because his is a second-best position itself.

The next subsection of this final chapter is called "Approaching the Cultist on the Intellectual Level." Hoekema gives several "general suggestions," followed by several "specific suggestions." "We must approach the cultist with genuine love. Though we may never love his errors, we must love him as a person." Good counsel, very difficult to follow. Most of us have trouble distinguishing the believer from the belief, the sinner from the sin, the nut from the nuttiness. But we have to do our best.

We should understand, says Hoekema, that "our primary purpose, however, may never be to defeat the cultist in argument or to demolish his position, but to win him for Christ."

He goes on to say—tellingly—that "the cultist has been taught that the members of regular churches regard him with hostility; the most effective way to disabuse him of that notion is to reveal a loving concern quite different from what he has been led to expect. This implies, needless to say, that we must never lose our tempers during the encounter but must remain calm and self-controlled."

Hoekema goes on to say that "we should approach the cultist with humility. We can be on the right side yet be incapable of representing it rightly. We can know the truth yet not pass it along intelligibly. We can assume rashly that right knowing necessarily implies able teaching, but we have to work at learning to teach. Such skill doesn't come automatically." Then, he says, "We must know the teachings of the cult." The trick is in being fair to those teachings. The temptation is to so simplify them that they become caricatures. If the cultist won't recognize his faith in our description of it, how can we expect him to be moved by what we then say about it?

Next come Hoekema's specific suggestions. It is here that the Catholic reader will find the greatest weaknesses.

"Face the question of your source of authority," insists Hoekema. "If you are talking to a Mormon, you must first show him from the Bible, which he does recognize as a sacred book, that Scripture itself teaches its own sufficiency and condemns the attempt to add other sources of revelation to it." There are two problems here. The Mormon has an out. He realizes the Book of Mormon doesn't square with the Bible. His solution is simple: "The Bible has been mistranslated wherever it contradicts the Book of Mormon." If he works from that premise, no listing of contradictions will convince him of the spuriousness of the Book of Mormon.

That's one problem. The other is a problem with Hoekema's own position. The fact is that the Bible nowhere claims to be sufficient as a rule of faith. Paul writes that it is "profitable," not sufficient (2 Tim. 3:16). Coming from a Reformed position, Hoekema naturally dismisses Tradition, in the proper Catholic sense, as being non-existent. He can see only "traditions of men." Notice his reference to "other sources of revelation." In Hoekema's mind these sources include the Book of Mormon, the writings of Mary Baker Eddy and Ellen G. White, and Catholic Tradition.

Even though the Bible isn't the sole rule of faith, much good can come from comparing what it says with what these other religions teach. This is especially true when one speaks with Jehovah's Witnesses since they don't recognize as inspired any books other than the Bible. (Christian Scientists say they don't regard Mrs. Eddy's writings as inspired, and Adventists say the same about Mrs. White's writings, but in practice these works are put nearly on a par with Scripture.)

Hoekema says the Christian should "present the evidence for the major doctrines of the Christian faith." He immediately runs into a conundrum. Which doctrines are these? Not the ones that "set your denomination apart from other Christian denominations" but the doctrines "which are held in common by all Evangelical Christians." Unfortunately, if that is what is to be presented, a kind of "mere Evangelical Christianity," then there won't be much to be said. The sad fact is that even Evangelicals are divided on doctrine. A faith built only on those few doctrines on which they all agree would be a thin, unsatisfying faith: little sustenance for a child, not remotely enough for an adult.

"Stick to the major doctrines," says Hoekema. "Do not allow yourself to be sidetracked into discussing minor issues." Well, what is a minor issue for one man may be a major issue for another. There are many people whose problems with respect to Catholicism can be reduced to a single issue—and that issue a minor one. If it isn't dealt with, no progress can be made. Infant baptism isn't among your top ten issues, you say? It is for some people. For some this issue must be resolved before any further illumination is possible. If you sidestep infant baptism when it's brought up, claiming it's too insignificant for notice, some minds will close.

Hoekema always counsels "direct appeal to Scripture." This is important but not always adequate. On many things Scripture speaks with an unclear voice or is entirely silent. You have to look elsewhere for support. One good place is early Christian history, including the history of dogmas and the history of practices or customs. Through such history we discover what early Christians believed, and we may infer from their belief what the apostles taught. Did Ignatius of Antioch believe in a hierarchy and the Real Presence? Then we may conclude he was taught them by John the Evangelist, whose student he was, and John, of course, learned directly from the Messiah.

The last two admonitions made by Hoekema are worth remembering: "Follow up the contact made" and "Keep on praying." A single conversation is almost never enough to effect a conversion, and no number of conversations, no amount of instruction, will work without prayer. These are good points from a Protestant writer from whom a Catholic can learn much, even while disagreeing on much.

Our Personal Mother

Over dinner, a U.S. Navy chaplain was recounting his experiences at what might be called an interdenominational spiritual pep rally where the featured speaker was a well-known television preacher. During a break in the proceedings, a minister sitting next to the chaplain leaned over and asked in a serious tone, "Have you accepted Jesus as your personal Savior?"

"Yes, I have," replied the chaplain. Without missing a beat he added, "And have you accepted Mary as your personal mother?"

The minister's jaw slackened. When he recovered his composure he said, "I never thought of it like that." Most people haven't. A little reflection will show that a personal relationship with Jesus should result in a personal relationship with his mother, and *vice versa.* If it doesn't, something's missing, and one's attitude toward Jesus is probably wrong.

When we look at what has happened recently, we see that as some Catholics increased their devotion to Christ (highly commendable and absolutely necessary in itself, of course), they decreased their devotion to Mary, perhaps on the theory that what is given to Mary is taken from Jesus. This might be called "the fixed-sum view of love," the idea being that there is only a definite amount so that to give some to A is to take an equal amount from B. This is a child's view of love, the view of a child who is worried that he will lose his parents' affection to the extent the new baby gets it. Parents know this isn't so. In fact, the reverse is true. The new child not only gets a full measure of love, but, in some inexplicable way, there seems to be even more parental love available for the older child than before. It is a mysterious case of the parts outstripping the whole.

In the same manner, devotion to Jesus does not have to be protected by minimizing or eliminating devotion to Mary. Heightened devotion to the Mother of God results, in practice, in heightened devotion to the Son of God. When devotion to Mary falters, in the long run devotion to her Son will decline. This is usually due to an underlying misconception about Christ.

One might say the unease about giving devotion to Mary stems from a latent Nestorianism, an objection to thinking of her as *Theotokos* (literally "God-bearer," the Mother of God). This objection, in turn, comes from confusion regarding the personhood of Christ. When we look at that heresy, we see that Nestorians explained their objection to the title "God-bearer" by saying, in a roundabout way, that Christ was not one divine Person in two natures but a moral unity of two distinct persons, one divine and one human. The logical outgrowth of *that* is reduced devotion to Jesus, because he is seen principally as man, not as God-man, and Mary is regarded as the mother of the man Jesus, not as the Mother of God.

Admittedly, talk about an old theological aberration takes us rather far afield from everyday life. One doesn't hear much talk on the streets about Nestorianism. Objections to the veneration of Mary are phrased differently: devotion to Mary is suitable only for priests (who are expected to engage in that kind of thing), elderly widows, and fuddy-duddies, or devotion to Mary and the saints is restricted to ethnic minorities— culturally backward people who must be allowed their relics on the past—or to people whose religious instincts are not well developed.

Yet there is in America a renewed interest in the Virgin and the saints, and it cuts across all levels of the Church. Much of it stems from Catholics' heightened interest in the Bible. From reading Scripture they understand our Lord to be more than just "out there," more than just an abstraction, and they seek a close and personal relationship with him. The interest in Jesus as an actual, historical person—and really God, not just a man—excites an interest in his mother—also a real, historical person—and, ultimately, in the whole notion of the communion of saints, even if that term is not used. The result is renewal of Marian devotions.

Some years ago, a few laymen started a rosary day in my city. It was a small affair, anachronistic to some, ignored by most, but it caught on. Three years later the organizers needed a football stadium, so large was the crowd—and what a crowd! It was not the geriatric set. To be sure, gray hairs were there, but the young were well represented as well—teenagers, college students, young marrieds—and they had not been induced to attend under threat of parental displeasure. They were present because they wanted to be. It is commonly thought such gatherings occurred only before Vatican II. Has the clock been turned back? In a way it has, and all to the good. A little reaction, now and then, benefits the soul, particularly when it puts in its right place something that was unthinkingly shunted aside.

Churchianity

Churchianity vs. Christianity is a comic book published by a Christian commune in Geelong, Australia, a suburb of Melbourne. The publishers identify themselves as "radical, unorthodox, living-by-faith Christians." "We're a small group of people who live together. We wrote and illustrated this booklet ourselves. We believe in things like love, faith, and honesty. We spend our lives trying to make the world a better place. Other than that, we're pretty normal people." Their chief bugaboo is "religion," by which they mean anything institutional, including, of course, the Catholic Church. The comic book purports to be a rephrasing of Paul's letter to the Galatians. Most panels contain cross-references to the appropriate line of that epistle. The problem is that these people, who "believe in things like love, faith, and honesty," are dishonest in their presentation.

Consider the first two panels. Paul (depicted as a bearded fellow with glasses) presents Titus to a "Churchianity" congregation. "Titus, my companion at this time, hadn't even been 'baptized.' And yet no one forced him to be ... although some tried! (2:3–4)." But this is what Galatians actually says (RSV): "But even Titus, who was with me, was not compelled to be circumcised, though he was a Greek." These Australians incorrectly equate circumcision with baptism, but Paul's point in this chapter is that he "had been entrusted with the gospel to the uncircumcised," the Gentiles, while Peter's main focus was the circumcised, the Jews (Gal. 2:7–8).

The cartoon Paul says, "The way I see it, Christ never told us to 'baptize' with water! ... That's a hangover from your religious past.*" But look at John 3:5: "Truly, truly, I say to you, unless one is born of water and the Spirit, he cannot enter the kingdom of God." This can only mean water baptism. Jesus doesn't say to be born *only* of the Spirit—he says "water *and* the Spirit." Despite what some claim, he does not mean by "water" the water of childbirth; the term is never used that way in the New Testament. Besides, look what he does right after this discourse: "Jesus and his disciples went into the land of Judea; there he remained with them and baptized" (John 3:22). This probably means not that Jesus himself performed baptisms (John 4:1–3), but that his disciples performed them at his direction. He must have told them to do so—a fairly clear proof that he "told us to 'baptize' with water."

The asterisk in the last sentence quoted from the comic book leads us to three verses: 1 Corinthians 1:17, John 1:33, and John 4:2. These, we are to believe, demonstrate that Jesus opposed water baptism. But here's what the verses really say:

"For Christ did not send me to baptize but to preach the gospel, and not with eloquent wisdom, lest the cross of Christ be emptied of its power" (1 Cor. 1:17). Does this mean baptism is to be opposed? Not at all. As *A New Catholic Commentary on Holy Scripture* states, "one must hear God's word before it can be accepted and one can be baptized." Paul was writing not against baptism but against an *unprepared* baptism, which reduces baptism from a sacrament to a magical incantation. Jesus himself said to preach first, *then* baptize: "Go therefore and make disciples of all nations [that is, preach to them first] baptizing them in the name of the Father and of the Son and of the Holy Spirit" (Matt. 28:19).

"I myself [John the Baptist] did not know him; but he who sent me to baptize with water said to me, 'He on whom you see the Spirit descend and remain, this is he who baptizes with the Holy Spirit'" (John 1:33). Again, no repudiation by Jesus of baptism. The opposite, in fact. John the Baptist had been performing a non-sacramental baptism, the baptism of repentance.

It was symbolic only. The baptism that Jesus instituted was sacramental baptism because through it one received the grace of the Holy Spirit. (A sacrament is a physical sign which signifies *and* effects the transmission of grace.)

"... although Jesus himself did not baptize, but only his disciples" (John 4.2). An apparent contradiction to John 3:22? Yes, but only apparent. Look at the full sentence: "Now when the Lord knew that the Pharisees had heard that Jesus was making and baptizing more disciples than John (although Jesus himself did not baptize, but only his disciples), he left Judea and departed again to Galilee" (John 4:1–3). All this says is that Jesus himself didn't perform baptisms—but he certainly approved of them.

In another series of frames the Australians reject the "bondage of Churchianity," relying on Galatians 4:31–5:1, but they misconstrue what Paul means. (He is talking about the Law and contrasting its salvific power with that of Christian faith.) The comic book refers to 1 John 4:7 ("love is of God, and he who loves is born of God and knows God"), suggesting the Church is not necessary—love is sufficient. But to love God fully is to love him the way he wishes, through his Church, which is his Mystical Body and which was established by him precisely as the "pillar and foundation of the truth" (1 Tim. 3:15). "Don't get sucked back into churchy games," say the Australians: "To hell with your sacraments." But these sacraments are Christ's and are from him. To reject them (and the ministers of them) is to reject him (Luke 10:16).

This brings us to another panel. The frustrated Paul sees a vast plot, and his Australian handlers cap the argument by saying, "church leaders should not use titles like 'Father,' 'Pope,' 'Reverend,' etc." (Matt. 23:9–10). But the real Paul uses just such a title for *himself.* "I became your father in Jesus Christ through the gospel" (1 Cor. 4:15). He uses the title "Father" exactly the way we use it now—for a spiritual father. By implication he approves of the title "pope" since the word come from the Greek and means "papa." Our biological father generates us, comforts us, feeds us, and cares for us in illness. At the spiritual level our spiritual father does the same. He generates a new, spiritual life in us at baptism, he comforts us in confession, he feeds us with the Eucharist, and he cares for our illness in the anointing of the sick.

What's frustrating about this comic book is not the impact it may have. What's frustrating is that it is an exemplar of a whole way of thinking. Lots of Christians chuck historic Christianity for a vague reading of the Bible. They reduce the gospel to a few pat phrases, leaving out the hard organizational sayings even when they accept most of the hard moral sayings. Superficially their Christianity is strong. They are zealous, and their zeal attracts others, particularly the down-and-out who have had their fill of "rules."

But real Christianity is full Christianity. It accepts everything Christ taught, not just the convenient parts, and it accepts human nature as it really is. Our Lord told us what the Church would be like: a field of good grain mixed with tares. In other words, it would be just like the Catholic Church, containing both the elect and the reprobate (Matt. 13:24–40). Many of the leaders of the Church would be grains of wheat and the very best grains, but some would be tares. This so scandalizes some people that they don't readily accept Jesus' words. They rebel by remaking Christianity according to their own preferences. They take all the structure, all the incarnationalism, out of it, hoping to take out also all the evil, not knowing that they can take out all the evil only if they take out all the Christians.

Churchianity vs. Christianity is symptomatic of what some might call the anti-intellectual element within Evangelical Christianity. Fortunately, this element does not affect most

Evangelicals, but it affects enough of them that today it affects even many Catholics. In many ways the dogmatic Fundamentalist is easier to reach than the anti-institutional Christian, the kind whose faith is best expressed through comic books.

Scholars Need Not Apply

From Macon, Missouri (population 6,000 and just down the road from the towns of Ethel, Elmer, and Excello), comes a tract titled *Correcting the King James Bible.* It's published by a ministry called The Flaming Torch, which also publishes tracts such as *Jehoshaphatelian Fundamentalism, Scholarolatry,* and *Did Our Inspired Bible Expire?* The author is W. Bruce Musselman, Jr.

He begins by saying that the "King James Bible is being attacked daily by Roman Catholics, Jehovah's Witnesses, Mormons, Modernists, Evangelicals, and Fundamentalists." (Apparently he considers himself not just a Fundamentalist, but a *real* Fundamentalist.) "The average Christian is given a King James Bible and told it is the Word of God. From then on he hears a steady stream of criticism of it through the radio, Christian books, magazines, in church, and in Christian schools. Anyone professing to have an ounce of education and who claims to be Godly and dedicated now assumes the right to correct the Bible any time it doesn't measure up to his beliefs and standards. The King James Bible is corrected by saying 'the original says' when no one has the original. It is also corrected by saying 'the Greek says' when there are a dozen conflicting Greek texts on the market. Others say 'this is an unfortunate translation' or 'a better reading is' when they don't know enough about Greek or manuscript evidence to know what they are talking about."

Then we get to the meat, which is collected into sixteen propositions. Consider a few of them.

1. "Correcting the Authorized Bible teaches infidelity. The preacher or teacher who professes to believe the Bible and then corrects it has just taught his students that the Bible has

errors in it and cannot be trusted." The problem with which Musselman never grapples is that the King James Version was an imperfect translation of an imperfect Greek text. It's not surprising, then, that errors occur in it, but he writes as though the English itself is somehow inspired. Indeed, he ends his tract with the statement that "Correctors of the Authorized King James Bible deny God has given his people his words in the English language exactly as he wanted them given." As it stands, this statement is true. Correctors do deny this because translations are not, in themselves, inspired—and Musselman seems to be referring to inspiration when he states the English words turned out "exactly as [God] wanted them given."

2. "Correcting the Authorized King James Bible reinstates the Roman Catholic Bible." Now we get to his problem. Musselman complains that Catholic Bibles rely on the manuscript known as Vaticanus, so named because it reposes in the Vatican. This manuscript is faulty, says Musselman, because it was one of those composed by "the apostate Alexandrian school in the third and fourth centuries." Somewhat contradictorily, he says that "Catholic translations are taken from [the] corrupt Bible" that was translated by Jerome—that is, from the Vulgate.

In the past most Catholic translations, it is true, were based on the Vulgate, but recent ones, such as the *New Jerusalem Bible* and the *New American Bible,* which are Catholic translations widely used in this country, have been based on the Greek and Hebrew, and even translations from the Vulgate, such as Msgr. Ronald Knox's, have made use of the original tongues. So, on the one hand, Musselman warns against anything based on the Vulgate. On the other, he warns against anything based on Vaticanus, which Jerome apparently didn't use.

Musselman complains that "Vaticanus leaves out most of Genesis and all of the New Testament after Hebrews 9:14." Aha! A faulty manuscript and one not to be trusted—one that's been doctored! But does this follow? Why are the beginning and end of the Bible missing from Vaticanus? Was it because the copyist disbelieved in what those books taught and so dropped them from his copy? No. They're missing because the manuscript is old and falling apart, and the two ends got lost (or simply crumbled away) over the centuries.

3. "Attacking the Authorized King James Bible repudiates the Protestant Reformation." That may or may not be so—probably not, since most conservative Protestants, people who show no particular love for the Catholic faith and never have entertained an uncharitable thought about the Reformation, use English translations other than the King James or alongside the King James. Such use may constitute "attacking the Authorized King James Bible" to Musselman, but none of these people would agree to that. They'd just tell you they're trying to use a more accurate translation.

4. "Correctors of the King James Bible take the same position as the Roman Catholic priest. The Catholic priest sets himself up as an authority over the Bible and encourages the people to listen to him rather than the Book. The teacher or preacher who corrects the Bible sets himself up as the authority for people to listen to, rather than the Bible, just like the priest. No wonder Bible reading is done by so few." (Keep in mind that this tract is intended mainly for "Bible Christians," Fundamentalists and conservative Evangelicals who may read nothing but the Bible.)

Do priests, teachers, and preachers set themselves "over" the Bible? If he means that they interpret the Bible, the answer is yes. After all, a sermon or homily, whether Catholic or Protestant, usually deals with the meaning of the text for the day. Musselman is of the view, shared by many, that understanding the Bible takes no intellectual effort. The meaning of a verse is supposed to jump out at you, and the meaning will be perfectly clear. This sounds fine in theory. The only trouble with it is that it breaks down in practice. Brother This and Sister That will repair to their Bibles at the conclusion of the service and will discover two distinct understandings of one verse. What's the sensible thing for them to do? Why, they turn to someone more experienced and, presumably, with a better understanding of Scripture. They turn to their minister.

5. "Correctors of the Authorized King James Bible reject the wisdom of God." What Musselman means is that the King James Version must be accurate because it "works." Missionaries have used it to convert millions, so it *must* be an entirely accurate translation. Of course, before 1611, when the King James Version appeared, there were other translations, such as the Vulgate, and these, too, resulted in the conversion of millions. There have been translations into languages other than English—for instance, Luther's German version and the German versions that preceded his—and these, too, resulted in millions of conversions. Which translation may claim the most? The King James Version can claim a large chunk of English-speaking Protestants, but not all. It can claim almost no Catholics, no Eastern Orthodox, and none of those Protestants who read no English. In other words, it can't claim to have been the instrument of conversion for the majority of Christians.

6. "Correctors of the Authorized Bible have no final authority. They appeal to the original no one has or can have. They believe, like Einstein's theory of relativity, that everything is relative and that there is no absolute truth on this earth which a man can get his hands on." First of all, Musselman has no idea what Einstein's theory means. It has nothing to do with

the notion that "everything is relative" or that "there is no absolute truth." Second, why set up a particular translation as the "final authority"? One wonders how many Frenchmen, including French Protestants, believe that only the English language King James Version is the "real" Bible.

7. "Correctors of the Authorized Bible put Christian scholarship above the God-authorized Bible. ... While professing to believe the Bible, many schools, including Evangelical and Fundamental, have accepted Christian education as the final authority and believe it has the right to sit in judgment on any Bible, Hebrew, Greek, or English." What it comes down to—and it's not a pleasant thought—is that in Musselman's religion one must abdicate the use of the critical faculties.

Whenever we pick up a Bible, of whatever translation or in whatever edition of the Hebrew and Greek, we first, before doing anything else, must exercise our minds and ask ourselves: "Is this as accurate a copy of the original writings as I can get? Can I rely on this to be faithful, so far as possible, to the originals?" Of course, we don't spend much time on such questions because most of us aren't capable of determining which versions are accurate and which aren't. We rely on experts to produce a text for us, and then we rely on the Church, ultimately, to interpret that text. In doing this we use our minds and we do, however indirectly, make use of solid scholarship. And that's just what we *should* do.

Musselman disagrees. He is suspicious of scholarship. He has seen it go awry, as it can, and he concludes it always goes awry. He is reduced to what is either bibliolatry or the thing next to it. He suffers from an immoderate devotion to a particular translation, coupled with a rejection of all others, coupled with the idea that it isn't even *possible* to have another translation as good or better. The problem with this is that readers of his tract might just buy his arguments. If they do,

69

they set themselves up for great disappointment. If they ever stumble across good, orthodox biblical scholarship, whether Catholic or Protestant, they'll be thrown for a loop. They'll discover the King James Version isn't specially anointed by God. Their confidence in the Bible may evaporate overnight. Having staked everything on an erroneous position, when they see that position crumble, they may see their faith crumble too.

Numbers Running

Some people are infatuated with dates. No, I'm not referring to the fruit of palms, and I don't mean taking in a movie with someone of the opposite sex. I mean numbers, as in years. Some folks like nothing better than to juggle dates and "prove" all sorts of things through apparent coincidences—which they see as more than coincidences. For instance, great import is given to the fact that Thomas Jefferson and John Adams died on July 4, 1826, the fiftieth anniversary of the Declaration of Independence. Some people see in this a divine warrant for the American political system, as though the Declaration were inspired, the political equivalent of Scripture.

When a Christian is infatuated with dates, his infatuation usually has something to do with the Last Days. I came across an old booklet that argued that "the day of the Lord is near"— much nearer than many might wish. It was supposed to have come in 1992, claimed the author, Jay R. Schmarje. How did he know this? From Catholic history.

Schmarje apparently dislikes anything that smacks of ecumenism, but not because he fears some brands of ecumenism might be bad for the Catholic faith. He's no Catholic, and he doesn't care what happens to Catholicism as such. His interest in the Church springs from his view that Catholicism will unite with Eastern Orthodoxy and Protestantism to form a One World Church that will be in service to the Antichrist. We are not to think of the partners in this ecumenical enterprise as equals, says Schmarje. The ringleader is Catholicism.

It all started in 962, when the German king, Otto I, was crowned Emperor of the Holy Roman Empire by Pope John XII. In that act a religious and spiritual leader united forces with a political and military leader. The result was the papacy becoming subject to the temporal power. This situation, says Schmarje, lasted until 1962. On "October 20, 1962 the first official act of the Second Vatican Council ended what had begun in 962," as Pope John XXIII called for discussions on reunion with non-Catholic churches. By addressing himself to all men, not just to Catholics, the Pope began the process of forming the One World Church.

Schmarje quotes Revelation 20:7–8: "And when the thousand years are expired, Satan shall be loosed out of his prison, and shall go out to deceive the nations which are in the four quarters of the earth, Gog and Magog, to gather them together to battle: the number of whom is as the sand of the sea." Note that one thousand years passed from Otto's coronation to John XXIII's call for reunion discussions. What does this imply? Yes, that the popes have been released from their subservience to the temporal power and are (and always have been) in the service of Satan, but it implies more than that, if we look at other facts. It implies the end is imminent.

Schmarje notes that the beginning of the first Gospel tells us there were 42 generations from Abraham to Christ. Since, by his reckoning, there were 1,050 years from Abraham to Christ, each generation was 25 years long. That's fact number one. Fact number two is that "Jerusalem shall be trodden down of the Gentiles, until the time of the Gentiles be fulfilled" (Luke 21:24). Jerusalem stopped being "trodden down" in 1967, with Israel's victory in the Six-Day War. Now to fact number three. Luke 21:32 says that "this generation shall not pass away, till all be fulfilled." If we add 25 to 1967, we get 1992. So 1992 was supposed to be the year when the prophecies in the last book of the Bible were played out.

Isn't this amazing?

Yes, and it's more than amazing. It's ludicrous. First of all, the Holy Roman Empire was not started with the coronation of

Otto I in 962. As every literate schoolboy knows, it began on Christmas Day, 800, when Charlemagne was crowned the first Holy Roman Emperor by Pope Leo III. One thousand years from 800 is 1800, and what happened in 1800? Nothing of consequence, apparently, or at least nothing that could be used in Schmarje's numerology. (Curiously, the Holy Roman Empire did last a millennium—and six years extra—finally being dissolved in 1806, but 1806 doesn't fit into Schmarje's calculations either.)

All this throws out the papacy as the focus of eschatological evil and Vatican II as the event that started the countdown toward Doomsday. But let's pretend 1962 did, indeed, mark the end of papal bondage to political powers. (A better date would be 1870, when the Papal States were absorbed by Italy and Pope Pius IX became "the prisoner of the Vatican.") What about Schmarje's other claims?

A serious problem rests with the period from Abraham to Christ. We are unsure of the dates of Christ's birth and death. Most commentators say he was born between 6 B.C. and 4 B.C., but perhaps as early as 8 B.C. and perhaps as late as 1 B.C. His death occurred either in A.D. 30 or A.D. 33. Which date is Schmarje using in his calculations? He doesn't say. If he's unsure about which date regarding Christ to choose for purposes of calculation, he should be still more unsure about choosing a date for Abraham. Many scholars say Abraham lived around 1850 B.C., but they admit they could be as much as a century off. With such imprecision at both ends of the spectrum, how does Schmarje come up with 1,050 years separating Christ from Abraham? He doesn't let us in on that.

For the sake of argument, let's grant Schmarje's notion that the 42 generations mentioned in Matthew 1 turned out to average 25 years in length. Let's grant that the length of one generation, 25 years, should be tacked on to the year that Israel stopped being "trodden down," if we're to get the year of the End Times. But why choose 1967? Modern Israel was founded in 1948, after a successful war. Israel fought another war in 1956, then a third in 1967, then a fourth in 1973, all against invading Arab states. Why single out 1967? Schmarje doesn't say. Of course, 1948 and 1956 wouldn't do, since adding 25 to them yields 1973 and 1983, years that had passed for Schmarje without sign of any final denouement. Why not add 25 to 1973? That would give 1998, in which case we would have two possibilities: 1992, which Schmarje prefers, and 1998. Which is the right one? Schmarje comes up with further calculations—for instance, he adds 30 to 1962 because Jesus was said to be "about thirty years of age" (Luke 3:23), and the result is, again, 1992. Schmarje gets the "confirmation" he seeks. (In any case, 1998 turned out not to be the right year either.)

One could go on, as he goes on, but you get his drift. Just keep in mind that this is a game anyone can play. Let's see what numerology, as conducted by Catholics, might yield.

In 535 began the Three Chapters dispute. The Three Chapters were theological writings that presented a questionable Christology. In 1535 Henry VIII declared himself head of the Church of England, and the Reformation in England was formalized. Notice that a thousand years separated these events, the first representing confusion regarding Christ, the second representing confusion regarding the Church. Henry's act sealed the success of the Reformation in Northern Europe, and, as we all know, many things have gone downhill since then. Shall we say, mimicking Schmarje, that Satan therefore was unleashed in 1535?

Now to Israel. General Allenby liberated Palestine from Arab rule in 1918. That's our starting point. If we add 25 years to 1918, we get 1943. That year marked the turning point of

World War II and the beginning of the downfall of the greatest modern enemy of the Jews, Hitler. See how it all fits together?

What do these calculations prove? That the Last Days passed us by, in 1943, and we didn't even know it? That the Antichrist was born in 1943 and will make himself known any time now? That the Cubs are going to win the World Series this year? No, all they prove is that we shouldn't pay much attention to numerology such as Schmarje's.

Left Behind

If you're of a certain age, you will remember when many Christians were worked up about the looming rapture, when faithful Christians would be taken up to heaven and everyone else would be left to stew on Earth. The rapture is out of fashion as a topic of conversation, but it may reappear as new generations of Evangelicals decide that Scripture has secrets just waiting to be unlocked by able interpreters.

Of all the failed rapture predictions, my favorites were by someone you likely never heard of: Edgar C. Whisenant (1932–2001). He is best known for *88 Reasons Why the Rapture Will Be in 1988*, which sold 4.5 million copies. The foreword explained that Whisenant's background

> includes five degrees in technical fields, and he is an electrical engineer by trade. Edgar's name is listed on the plaque of people who helped put the first man on the moon; he is retired from NASA. His experience also includes being an instructor at the Naval Academy (Annapolis). Having the desire put in his heart by God to find the end-time solution, he set out to do it as any engineer would. His work was done methodically, and honestly, with no denominational bias.
>
> His approach for the study of Scriptures was done logically, knowing all events were sequential and had to fit in such a way as to verify and interlock with all other Bible prophecy. Edgar has never had any biblical training from any Bible schools, just his own research, which I might add was six to 14 hours every day for almost ten years."

Reading Whisenant's short book, one suspects most of those hours were spent not reading the Bible but playing with equations. Two examples must suffice. Reason 44 in *88 Reasons Why the Rapture Will Be in 1988* includes these proofs:

"From 2422 B.C., we have the instruction for building the Ark given by God to Noah. Thus 2422 B.C. + (9x490) = 1988, the year of the Church's rapture. Thus, 490 years is a period of dealing with a people (7x70 or 70 weeks [of 7 days]), and 9 is 3x3, the number of God; therefore, 9x490 is the end of God's dealing with the Gentile people from Noah to the end of the time of the Gentiles in 1988."

"From 532 B.C., the start of the Jewish punishment seven times over for not obeying God, or a punishment of 2,520 years (Lev. 26:14–39); or from 602 B.C. when Daniel told Nebuchadnezzar his dream of the idol with the head of gold, subtract the 70-year Babylonian captivity and you have 532 B.C. + (7x360) = 1988, the year of the Church's rapture."

There are many other equations, several more just within reason 44. Whisenant lists "important numbers in the Bible," giving the symbolism behind 3, 7, 24, 30, 40, 49, 70, 90, 180, 280, 360, 490, 1,000, 2,520, and other numbers. Then he manipulates these until he comes up with the proper year for the rapture. More than that, he narrows it down to two days (Rosh Hashana), and he goes on to pinpoint wars, the Second Coming, and every other event mentioned in Revelation.

You'll note the first of the two proofs given above depends on our knowing that Noah was told to build the ark in 2422 B.C. How does Whisenant know this date? Not from the Bible, which nowhere lists it. Scholars can give us the century in which Abraham lived—that's as precise as most say they can get—and Abraham lived near the beginning of recorded history, which means it becomes impossible to determine dates more than a few centuries prior to Abraham. But what if you go all the way back to Noah? We have no way of knowing just when he lived—and we'd have to know not just to the century, but at least to the year if Whisenant's proof were to work.

But Whisenant wasn't worried. He knew when Noah lived. An engineer, he did what any good engineer would do. He calculated it. He worked backward and determined that creation occurred in 4005 B.C. (differing with the venerable James Ussher, the Calvinist archbishop of Armagh, who calculated in the seventeenth century that creation occurred in 4004 B.C.). Whisenant determined that Jesus was born on September 29, 4 B.C. (a secret kept from all scholars until now) and that the key date for modern history was May 14, 1948, when the state of Israel was established. After that, it was child's play.

Of course, Whisenant had a little help. He relied on Meir Kahane, the rabble-rousing rabbi who, before his assassination, sat in the Knesset. From Kahane's writings Whisenant learned the importance of the number 40. He also relied on "a famous psychic [who] said that a great world leader was born at sunrise, February 5, 1962. This person may be a likely candidate for the Antichrist. It appears that Satan's events start at sunrise and God's at sunset." Who was this psychic? Whisenant is coy about it, but it appears to have been Jeanne Dixon, a nominal Catholic who believed in reincarnation and who survived as a reputable prognosticator despite a remarkably consistent record of inaccurate predictions.

Jeremiah's Lament

One of my favorite books that I have never finished reading is *Romanism: A Menace to the Nation*, written by Jeremiah Crowley, a one-time Catholic priest. Published in 1912, the book has a thick purple cover with embossed gold lettering. Glued into a recess on the front is a drawing of Pope Pius X; beneath it are the lines "Our Lord God the Pope" and "King of Heaven, Earth, and Hell." The title page describes the book as "a searchlight upon the papal system"; it contains "startling charges against individuals in the hierarchy made and filed by the author and a score of prominent priests with photographic proofs and illustrations."

The promotional words promise a lurid read—at least lurid by the standards of a century ago. It was just the kind of book that would appeal to a populace suspicious of Catholicism and worried about the large influx of immigrants from Catholic portions of Europe. (My maternal grandparents had immigrated just four years prior to the publication of *Romanism*. They were the kind of people—makers of the sign of the cross—who worried "real" Americans.)

What intrigues me most about Crowley's book is the frontispiece. The photograph shows him in a formal stance: full left profile, leaning against a table, a scroll in his right hand. His wavy hair is largely gray, his coat well-tailored. Part of an elegant watch chain is visible. His facial lines are rounded, not angular, belying his age but not his weight.

Halfway through the text he explains, "This book contains my photograph, and I state now that my height is six feet and three inches, and my weight is two hundred and fifty pounds." At the time of publication Crowley was 51. He was born in Ireland, ordained to the priesthood, and ended up imprisoned by Her Majesty's Government for reasons that, on a cursory reading, are unclear but probably justifiable. He left for America, settling in Chicago, where he was assigned to regular parish work, but he fell afoul of the hierarchy when he and other priests opposed the appointment of a new bishop, or so he says. He ended up excommunicated, but the excommunication may have been rescinded. I haven't read enough of the book to understand even his version of the story. What is clear, though, is that by 1906 he was lecturing against the parochial school system and alleged corruption in the clergy, focusing most of his attacks on the Archdiocese of Chicago.

What kind of a man was this who stares off a page printed so long ago? What was his real story? Perhaps the photograph gives a clue. What strikes me are the softness of his features and the finery of his clothes.

Crowley seems not to have been an ascetic. This is confirmed by an appeal he makes. "If I am to succeed," he says, referring to his public campaign, "I must have something more than kind wishes. I must have money! My opponents have wealth which runs into the millions. I cannot get needed publicity for the truth without money. How can I get money? The sale of a few million copies of my book would yield enough to secure a publicity of truth which will shake the Catholic world as with an earthquake." Ten pages later he laments, "The American clergy, high and low, exhibit an insatiable desire for money. They seek and obtain it in the sacred name of religion—for God and Holy Mother Church! Many of the means they employ to secure it are not only questionable but criminal." How many readers in 1912 saw the irony here? The clergy are rapacious, but Crowley wants only the proceeds from the sale of "a few million copies" of his book.

His words remind me of an episode recounted by Archbishop Fulton Sheen. At a retreat for priests, one of the clerics complained loudly and publicly about the Church's wealth. He insisted the Church sell off artworks, cash in investments, and give the proceeds to the poor. After the session the priest came up to Sheen and repeated his remonstrances. Sheen eyed him and asked, "How much did you steal?"

"What?" said the priest, indignant.

"How much did you steal?" repeated Sheen. The priest protested. Sheen asked again, "How much did you steal?" At length the priest admitted he had been taking money from the collection basket, his rationale being that, since the Church wasn't a good steward of wealth, he could put the money to better use than the hierarchy could.

I wonder whether there was some of this in Crowley, a man who protesteth too much. If ever afforded the leisure, I would like to spend a few days in the archives of the Archdiocese of Chicago, seeing if a coherent story could be pieced together. What happened to Jeremiah Crowley? Does anyone still live who may have known him in his old age, if he reached old age? Was he ever reconciled to the Church, or did he end his years as a front man for anti-Catholic forces unwilling to show their own faces? I hope someday to find out.

Other Books by Karl Keating

Apologetics the English Way

Can a reasonable case be made for Catholicism? A compelling case? Or does the Catholic argument falter before critiques from top-notch opponents? Judge for yourself. You don't have to be Catholic or even religious to relish the intellectual sparring that goes on in these pages. This is high-level controversial writing, culled from Karl Keating's favorite books. Each selection is a forceful exposition of Catholic truth. All come from English Catholics, and all are aimed at a single antagonist, with the public invited to look over the writer's shoulder.

These were men who knew the Catholic faith and could explain it to others. The individuals against whom they wrote may not have been converted—one or two were, in the long run—but any number of readers of these little-known masterpieces must have found their faith bolstered and their doubts assuaged. The issues covered in these exchanges are still discussed today—but probably nowhere in as glorious a style as here.

The New Geocentrists

Were Copernicus, Galileo, and Kepler wrong? Does the Earth orbit the Sun, or does the Sun orbit the Earth? For centuries, everyone thought the science was settled, but today the accepted cosmology is being challenged by writers, speakers, and movie producers who insist that science took a wrong turn in the seventeenth century. These new geocentrists claim not only that Earth is the center of our planetary system but that Earth is motionless at the very center of the universe.

They insist they have the science to back up their claims, which they buttress with evidence from the Bible and Church documents. But do they have a case? How solid is their reasoning, and how trustworthy are they as interpreters of science and theology? *The New Geocentrists* examines the backgrounds, personalities, and arguments of the people involved in what they believe is a revolutionary movement.

No Apology

Karl Keating has been a Catholic apologist for nearly four decades. In these pages he shares some of his own experiences and some stories from times past. He writes about how to do apologetics and how not to. He defends the very idea of apologetics against a theologian who thinks apologetics is passé. He looks at how the faith is promoted through beauty and through suffering. He takes you from his own backyard to such distant times and places as fifth-century Jerusalem and sixteenth-century Japan.

Anti-Catholic Junk Food

You are what you eat. That is as true of the mind as of the body. Eat enough greasy food, and your silhouette will betray your culinary preferences. Give credence to enough greasy ideas, and your mind will be as flabby as your waistline. This book looks at eight examples of religious junk food, things that have come across Karl Keating's desk during his career as a Catholic apologist. You likely will find these morsels unconvincing and unpalatable, as you should. The problem is that plenty of people—including people on your block—consider such stuff to be intellectual high cuisine.

Often, the best way to succeed at something is to learn how to fail at it—and then to avoid the things that lead to failure. There are books that tell you how to succeed at hiking Mt. Whitney. This book helps you *not* to fail by showing you what *not* to do, from the moment you start planning your trip to the moment you reach the summit. You learn what gear not to buy and not to take, how to maximize your chances of getting a hiking permit (don't apply for the wrong days of the week!), how to prepare yourself physically without over-preparing, how to avoid being laid low by altitude or weather problems, how not to take too much food or water—or too little. You even discover how to shave a mile off the trip by using little-known shortcuts that can make the difference between reaching the summit and reaching exhaustion.

Most people who depart the Mt. Whitney trailhead fail to reach the top. Some fail because of things entirely beyond their control, but many fail because of insufficient preparation, false expectations, and basic errors of judgment. Their mistakes can come at the beginning (such as failing to get a hiking permit), during the preparation stage (such as being induced to buy "bombproof" gear), or during the hike (such as not heeding bodily warning signs).

Through engaging stories of his own and others' failures, Karl Keating shows you how to fail—and therefore how to succeed—at hiking the tallest peak in the 48 contiguous states.

About Karl Keating

Karl Keating holds advanced degrees in theology and law (University of San Diego) plus an honorary doctor of laws degree (Ave Maria University). He founded Catholic Answers, the English-speaking world's largest lay-run Catholic apologetics organization. His best-known books are *Catholicism and Fundamentalism* (nearly a quarter-million paperback copies sold) and *What Catholics Really Believe* (about half that many sold). His avocations include hiking, studying languages, and playing the baroque mandolino. He lives in San Diego. You can follow him at his author website and on Facebook:

KarlKeating.com
Facebook.com/KarlKeatingBooks

www.ingramcontent.com/pod-product-compliance
Lightning Source LLC
Chambersburg PA
CBHW060529030426
42337CB00021B/4190